THE GLOW UP

the GLOW UP
Ascending in my Twenties

A MEMOIR

JAMILLA KABONGO

REVISED EDITION

Cover Photographer: Gurman Singh

Cover Designer: Donnie Ramsey; @donisdope

Interior Designer: Amanda Clarke; AClarke Editorial

All photographs are courtesy of Jamilla Kabongo-Bah

Hardcover ISBN: 978-1-0689486-0-2 | Softcover ISBN: 978-1-0689486-1-9 | Ebook ISBN: 978-1-0689486-2-6

Printed in the United States of America.

To my readers:
I hope you find this book inspiring &
garner the courage to heal.

Contents

December 19th, 2019: Out of all the moving dates in my first twenty-six years of life, this one sticks in my brain. It was the day my mother, brother, and I were given a third chance at creating a new life. The life we'd always envisioned.

Looking back was not part of the plan. I told myself, *Leave the past behind you!* But the notion that I could simply *be* without reflecting didn't last. I was unhappy but felt there was no reason to be. After all, I now had the external harmony I wanted: a new home, a new beginning. So, what was this melancholy?

I soon discovered that I could no longer run from the memories that plagued me. I had to part ways with the surface-level stuff. I had to dig deeper.

Boom. Boom. Boom. My stomach sank as I recalled the sound of Auntie Felicia thumping up and down the oak staircase in the family house to confront her siblings. *Crash!* My body trembled as I recalled the noise of the glass shattering on the kitchen floor when my grandmother threw it at my mother. "*Tu es stupide!*" My body curled up into a ball when I recalled hearing the words

Grandma shouted at Mommy when the police came to our front door.

Trauma is what I remembered. The things that shook me to the core. The things I had brushed off for years. The things I didn't want to face. But now that we had moved into a quieter place, it was time for me to face them.

I felt the urge to talk to my brother, Jonathan, who was twenty-one at the time. Out of everyone in my life, my younger brother was the only person who could understand the depth of my grief. We were the children who had seen everything: the aggression, abandonment, mistreatment, and verbal and physical violence.

"How did you heal from what we went through as children?" I asked him as we drove in his black Honda Civic. He paused for a moment and then glanced over at me. "Let's talk about it at the lake." Rap music shook the car and momentarily silenced the voice in my head.

We parked at the frozen lake around Port Credit and sat in his car. Jonathan turned the ignition off. Then he took a deep breath and said, "I wrote. That's what helped me when I was younger." My brother waved his long index finger in my direction. "You need to write, Jamilla!"

His advice was a sign. A *higher* sign. One that I saw as clearly as the blue sky.

I needed to nurture myself back to good health, and the most profound way I could do that was by looking inward. I had to start healing from my childhood wounds, especially the deepest one: the daddy wound. Only then could I truly allow myself to ascend.

I didn't plan to write a memoir. I just started writing about my day: my emotions, what I had learned, what I needed to work on, and then I gradually wrote about my wounds. I wrote in a purple Michael Jackson notebook I'd bought when I was twelve and never used. Perhaps I was saving those blank pages for the day I realized I had something paramount to write about.

Throughout this healing journey, my mom constantly told me, "Milla, use your pain for a purpose. God has heard our cries. It *wasn't* in vain. There is a purpose in our pain." I have found that purpose. It's to help others.

It's my prayer that the wounded inner child within each one of us is heard and eventually healed. To be healed could look like many different things. Sometimes you might even feel worse as you dig further into the past. But remember, as Renee Kapuku from the *To My Sisters* podcast so brilliantly says, "Your journey isn't meant to be linear; it's meant to be one of progress." Understand the main reason for your healing: to *free* yourself. We got this!

Light and Love,

Jamilla

Disclaimer: The stories and dialogue in this book are recounted to the best of the author's memory. To protect privacy and safety, some names and details of characters, locations, and situations have been altered, embellished, or presented in composite form. Highly sensitive and possibly triggering subjects such as domestic violence and suicidal ideation will be discussed.

One

DADDY WOUND

An absent father is like a book with missing pages, a story incomplete.

— Unknown

"Mom, do I have a dad?" I asked her after she tucked me into bed.

"Yes," she replied. The hesitancy in her voice was profound.

"Where is he? What happened to him?"

Mommy paused for a few seconds. "I … I don't know, Jamilla."

"What happened to him?" I repeated.

"Oh, Jamilla!" Mom screeched. "Why does it matter?"

I was six years old and starting to notice that my family looked a lot different from other families. Most of the kids at school had both a mom and a dad. I only had a mother. Where was my dad?

Mom squirmed on the side of my bed she was lying on. I could tell she didn't want to talk about him. I didn't care though. I wanted answers.

"Is he … dead?"

"No, no. He's alive." Mom took a deep breath. "He was … a *bad* guy."

I gasped. "A bad guy?" *No way!* The word "bad," to me, was synonymous with the villainous Marvel characters I'd seen on TV. It didn't make sense that Mommy would've been with someone like that. I didn't completely believe her.

"Promise you'll tell me everything when I'm sixteen," I said, rubbing my eyes.

"Okay." Mommy relaxed her shoulders and left the room. But she came right back. "Here," she said.

"What is it?" I asked her, reaching out my hand.

"A picture of your dad."

I looked deep into my father's dark brown eyes, and my heart warmed. Even though I couldn't remember his face, it was oddly familiar.

"Who are you?" I whispered.

After Mom shut my bedroom door, I jumped out of bed, grabbed a blue tack and pinned the picture above my bed. I wanted to see his face every day so I would never forget it again.

The next morning, the picture was gone.

* * *

For most of my life, no one said a word about my father. Not my mom, grandmother, aunts, or uncles. It was like he hadn't existed.

There was an invisible child safety lock on the door titled *Your Father*. From the night I first asked my mother about him, I couldn't enter no matter how hard I tried to crack the code. So I didn't bother.

But by the time I turned nine years old, not being able to probe my mom for answers made me angry and frustrated. My brother was upset with our mother's secrecy, too. "Who's my dad?" he asked her one afternoon.

My mom turned her back to us and started rearranging items on the bedside table. We were living with Grandma then, and the three of us shared a room.

"What's his name?" I asked.

Mom hesitated. "It's … Marcus … He was part Lebanese."

"Well, what else is there to know about him?"

"He named you," Mommy revealed.

My name always intrigued people, especially Muslim men and women in our neighbourhood. "Ah, your name is *Jamilla*. Do you know what it means?"

I nodded. I was too modest to say, *It means beautiful*.

"And you *are* your name," they'd say.

Then the Muslim man or woman's eyes would open wide. The hint of intrigue I'd see in their lingering gaze would tell me they wanted to know more.

"My dad is a quarter Lebanese," I would tell them. "I got the name from him."

As I got older, somehow the conversation about my name would turn to my dad's whereabouts. "Does he live in Canada?" was usually the next question. People would ask innocently, not knowing that there wasn't much for me to add.

"I don't know him," I'd tell them. Their jaws would drop. And I'd find myself squirming much like my mother did when I was six years old and asked her questions about my father for the first time.

"It's okay," I would assure them. "Don't feel sorry. You didn't know."

* * *

A few days before my sixteenth birthday, my dad must have been on my mother's mind. Perhaps she was feeling weighed down by the heavy load of raising two teenage children on her own. "Bay-bay, we're going to do this together," my dad had promised Mommy when she was pregnant with me.

Mom greeted my brother and me in the living room that morning and asked, "How do you feel about your dad?"

My body tensed up. *Why is she asking us this?* I thought. Looking back on it now, maybe this was God's funny way of reminding my mom and me about the vow we had made to each other years ago during our bedtime talk.

"How would we know?" Jonathan said on his way out. "We don't know much about him."

"Yeah, Mom! You promised to tell me everything about him when I turn sixteen."

Mommy sat on the couch while I stood with my arms crossed. What she said next was more than I could stomach. "My relationship with your dad was abusive. He got physical with me sometimes after you were born … You stopped going to him, and he blamed me for that. The relationship wasn't good."

"Really?"

"Yes," she answered without a twinkle in her eyes.

"I'm sorry to hear that, Mom," I said. "You don't have to tell me more."

I felt horrible. I didn't want to put my mom through the pain of remembering my father's violence towards her. Nor did I want to retraumatize myself.

Leave it alone! I wanted to protect my mother. *I'll make this sacrifice for her.*

But I couldn't entirely put the daddy topic to rest. There was a daddy-shaped hole in my heart that I carried deep within me. A hole that wouldn't go away no matter how much I tried to suppress the pain and pretend everything was okay. And so bit by bit, I pieced together the story.

Two

SWEET DAYS

Childhood is the one story that stands by itself in every soul.

— Ivan Doig

My story had a false beginning. At twenty-six years old, I know that. But before now, it went like this:

Mommy, Jonathan, and I lived in Aurora, a city in Ontario, Canada. Throughout the first two years of our lives on Bellarosa Lane, we resided in my grandmother's townhouse with my mom's siblings: Luke, Celeste, Felicia, and Rick, who she relied heavily on. Grandma was like my second mother. My aunts and uncles were like my older siblings.

The Kabongos were a close-knit family. From the day my grandparents and their five young children fled their homeland, the Democratic Republic of Congo, due to a civil war to finding themselves living on stable ground in England and then Canada, their bond remained unbreakable.

In those days, Auntie Celeste stepped up a lot. She relieved my mom, a twenty-one-year-old single mother, of the stress of raising not only one, but two young children. Whenever I was around Auntie Celeste, I was at ease. She had this ability to make me feel protected and safe. Strangely, I felt that she understood my high level of sensitivity. I could never understand why or how. But I'd seek refuge in her when I needed to.

One morning, my mom dressed me in a blue-and-white chequered dress and tied my hair in tight pom poms. We were going to church, and Mom was in a hurry.

"Come here," she demanded, sitting on the sofa in the living room. My mom slapped Vaseline over my face.

"*Ouch!*" I backed away. The pom poms hurt my head, and Mommy was applying lotion too harshly. On top of that, I didn't want to wear that silly dress.

"Stop moving," Mom shouted.

I stood still. When my mom finished spreading Vaseline on my skin, I saw Auntie Celeste's long, slender, ebony legs glide into the living room. I ran to her. She took my hand, and I stayed by her side until we left the house.

My family had a sense of comradery with the people outside of our home, too. We acquainted ourselves with a beautiful Eritrean family. Finding people in the neighbourhood who we could culturally relate to made us feel comfortable. It was a cultural shock for my relatives to be around so many non-Black people after coming from the Congo.

Their family consisted of a single mother, Fefe, and her three daughters: Ella, Fatimah, and Mary. Every now and then, we'd visit them to experience something outside of our mundane routine of being stuck in the house. We'd eat injera with stew and vegetables. Or Fefe would make her specialty: lasagna. That was my brother's favourite. "Jo-nah!" Fefe would shout. "I'm going to make lasagna for you."

That dish became so popular that my mom started watching her cook it. "What's the recipe?" Mom asked, standing beside Fefe over the hot stove. Now, Mommy is known for it, too.

I was drawn to Fatimah, a young woman with a svelte figure. For as long as I'd known her, she'd worn a large afro with pride, something most Black people were and still are too fearful to put on display. We'd rather not have to deal with people's curious eyes, having our hair touched without permission, or being asked why our hair stands up. I admired Fatimah for her beauty, but mostly, for being unapologetically herself.

Every time I saw Fatimah, she was filled with positive energy. It radiated from her. Being in her presence enlivened me. I felt like I was around my type of person. My tribe.

Before Fatimah and her family moved, she visited us. It would be the last time I'd see her. But her energy was no different.

Knock. Knock. "It's Fatimah!" she hollered.

My brother and I ran to the front door. "Hi Fatimah!" I shouted. Then I proceeded to show her how loose my tooth was.

"I think it's going to fall out tonight, Jammy!" she said, looking me in the eyes keenly.

"No … I don't think so," I responded, trying to hide the tooth I had just shown her.

When I woke up the next morning, the first thing I did was wiggle my tooth around. *Plop.* It fell out.

I flipped my small, white pillow on its backside and saw ten dollars. "Mommy, look!" I told her, holding the bill high. "The tooth fairy gave me $10!"

"I know," Mom said, grinning. "Fatimah left it for you last night."

I grabbed pencil crayons and paper, and made Fatimah a thank-you card.

Looking back, Fatimah was more than a tooth fairy. In embracing her own uniqueness, she made me believe that I could too, one day.

* * *

In mid-2001, my mother earned a college diploma in human resources while working as a sales representative at

Winners. Once she became financially stable, we rented a townhouse in the same complex as our relatives. We were fortunate to live near my mom's older brother, Luke, who was applying to university, her two younger sisters, Celeste and Felicia, who were retaking high school courses, and Rick, who was starting his sophomore year. My grandmother, a former nurse in the Congo and a recent widow, also returned to college to reobtain her nursing degree to support the family after Canada refused to recognize her foreign education and credentials.

The perceived beauty about immigrating to Canada, known for its multiculturalism and diversity, is that there is surplus opportunity available for everybody. One can build themselves up by setting goals and working hard. But there is oftentimes one con that can outweigh the many pros of living in a country free from constant volatility: starting from the bottom of the ladder, no matter how high you've already reached back in your native country.

After my grandma graduated from college at the age of forty-four and got a nursing job at a hospital in the Greater Toronto Area, she saved up money to purchase a house in the quiet city of Vaughan in early 2003. We stayed in Aurora, while my aunts and uncles relocated with her.

Mom didn't have a driver's licence or a car, and so, visiting our relatives regularly was difficult. Knowing that, Grandma would pick my brother and me up in her black Honda Accord and take us to Tim Hortons for a sprinkle or honey dip donut. She'd play Koffi Olomidé, a popular Congolese rumba artist. After we got our bite to eat, my brother and I would fall asleep to the melodic sounds and gentle vibrations of one of her favourite songs, "Choc."

"We're home," she'd tell us, shaking our legs. We'd wake up in a daze. "Really?"

One day after school, Grandma visited us unexpectedly. "Grandma, I want this new toy called a Tamagotchi," I told her. "Everyone has one."

"Okay, I'll take you to Toys R' Us after work on Tuesday," she promised me.

I chose a magenta Tamagotchi with sparkles on it. As we stood in line to buy it, Grandma said, "Okay, so we're getting your Tama-*gucci*."

I was embarrassed, so I politely corrected her. "Grandma, it's called a Tama*gotchi*," I whispered, giggling.

"Oh, who cares," she responded, light-heartedly. "I'm French!" We laughed so hard that I forgot I had been embarrassed.

* * *

Following my extended family's departure out of Aurora, my mom's best friends and closest confidants in our complex were Brandi, Gale, and Kelly. There was an immediate bond between them and my mother, one I didn't completely understand. But now I do. They were all survivors of domestic abuse.

Brandi, a modelesque Congolese lady with a newborn boy, was married to an abusive guy when Mom befriended her. "He was such a mean man," Mommy said, recalling the stories Brandi had told her about his short-temperedness. I remembered him, too. A skinny, well-dressed Black man with a fresh buzz cut, who barely said a word other than "hi" and "bye."

Gale, a wavy-haired white woman, had left her abusive husband and was raising her son, Luther, with the help of her parents. She and my mom met at an adult learning program. Mom wanted to do something in business, and Gale, a preacher's child, envisioned herself as a nurse.

Kelly, an ambiguous-looking woman with curly, dark brown hair, was of mixed heritage. Her mother was a petite Jamaican lady with a heavy accent, and her father was a white Canadian. That added another layer to their budding friendship: two Black women navigating their lives with young children around the same age.

We'd visit their unit to share a meal. Or my brother and I would play with Kelly's two daughters, Amelia and Emily, while our moms had their weekly girl chats.

"Girl, he did this to me," Mom would say, swirling her hot cup of peppermint tea.

"He said this to me," Kelly would confess, eating her famous rum cake.

What was dim to me then, at age six, I see more clearly now. Most of the women in our government-housing complex were single mothers from middle-class families who had found themselves in relationships with violent men, or with ones who didn't know how—or did want—to be a father. Their main goal was to find ways to better themselves and provide for their children. They found solace and strength in each other through bonding over their shared trauma.

Gale would ring on our doorbell if she needed sugar. Kelly would cook a jerk chicken dish or bake a cake and invite us over for dinner. My best friend, Katie, and her mom, Anita, would bring me clothes in large garbage bags when Katie outgrew them. Or Anita would patch up my wound when I was injured. It was a real sisterhood, one you rarely see anymore.

* * *

Katie was not only my best friend, she was like the sister

I never had. I took to her for two reasons: she was kind, and she was two years my senior. She was someone I looked up to.

My mom seemed to trust Katie and her mother, Anita. Anita's was the only unit in our complex where I was allowed to spend all day. Katie and I would make gimp bracelets, build a fort in her living room, or take turns playing a *SpongeBob Square Pants* game on her GameCube.

Once in a while, Katie would get annoyed with me. "Mom, she's doing it again," I'd overhear her say. I was more interested in the gaming systems than doing girl-like things with her. But my best friend wanted my full attention, something my ruminative and explorative mind found hard to give at times.

A conversation Katie had with her mother during one of our playdates would capture all my attention though. We never talked about the absence of our fathers throughout our friendship. But when I overheard their mother-daughter chat, I got a closer look into her life.

"Mom!" she hollered. "Dad promised he'd come see me this week."

"Katie, I can't force him to visit you," Anita replied.

"But … he promised!"

Anita was right. No one can or should force a parent to be a part of their child's life. It's something they must want to do. However, as children, it's hard for us to understand that. In Katie's mind, it was simple: her dad should see her whenever she asked.

That afternoon, Anita had trouble comforting Katie, who was crying. They went back and forth. Meanwhile I stood in the corner not knowing if I should help soothe Katie or stay mute.

"Jamilla, we'll have to postpone the playdate for another day," Anita told me. "Katie isn't feeling well."

I had just got to their unit, so I was disappointed. But I understood her decision.

"Okay, maybe we can get together next week," I responded, cheerfully. "I hope Katie's fine. Tell her I said goodbye!"

Whether it was hearing the agony in Katie's voice due to another one of her dad's broken promises, or the anger in Luther's voice after his father remarried and abandoned him, the feeling was the same: inconsistency was painful. And seeing how this type of pain negatively impacted and consumed my peers frightened me. The unhappiness that came from having their fathers in and out of their lives appeared far worse than what I was dealing with, so I didn't complain. As much as I was curious about who my father was, I was also content with my reality—having him away.

* * *

The rhythmic flow in my mother's household was consistent. Before the sun rose, from the day we rented our townhouse until the end of 2006, I'd wake up to the rich, weighty voice of Anita Baker. The sultry, calming voice of Sade. Or the soulful voices of Yolanda Adams and "Shackles" by Mary Mary.

Mom wasn't the best waker-upper. "Jamilla! Jonathan! Wake up!" she'd yell. I'd pretend I didn't hear her until I couldn't hold my position any longer. So, hearing soft music as I awakened put me in a more pleasant mood.

Jonathan and I would then head to a daycare near our townhouse with Mommy. From there Ms. Daphne, our bus driver from junior kindergarten until grade three, drove us to Parkdale Public School in a dark green minivan. She was an elderly white lady who'd suck the top of her mouth as if it was itchy. It always tickled me when

I'd hear her do it.

My closest friend at school was a curly-haired boy named Theo. It was so cute how he swirled his golden locks around his index finger. Plus, he was reserved and independent like me, drawing me more towards him.

Before our scheduled naps in junior and senior kindergarten, we'd listen to Pop music together on his small music player. "Here," he'd say, passing the device to me. "Pick a song." It made me happy whenever he'd let me choose the next tune to play.

After grade one, we drifted apart. We had fewer classes together and liked to do different things at recess. I liked to play soccer and hopscotch with my other friends Kai, Dean, and Paige. Theo liked to sketch or be by himself.

But at the book fair in grade two, Theo approached me. "What do you want?" he asked. I hesitated. *A book from the Joe Sherlock Kid Detective collection.*" He grabbed the book and handed the cashier a $20 bill. Afterwards, he gave me twenty-five cents to buy a vanilla cupcake with confetti icing on top, the best kind.

The book fair was a big deal. It was the rare occasion students had to buy fancy pencils, pens, erasers, books, and bookmarks. But it was also a clear indicator of how different my classmate's financial situations were in comparison to mine.

I never had money to purchase what I wanted on my wish list. The sparse change around the house told me Mommy didn't have extra money to spare. *I won't ask her*, I'd tell myself.

It wasn't the end of the world if I couldn't get what I wanted. But there was a big part of me that longed to have $5, $10, or even $20 to spend on whatever I wanted, like the kids from more well-off families did.

I still have the book Theo bought me. The way he treated me, a daddy-less little girl, meant a lot to me then and now.

* * *

When we weren't at school, my brother and I had the freedom to do whatever we wanted inside our unit before bedtime. We used to plead with Mommy about going to bed later than eight o'clock. But those were the rules.

My brother and I were extremely close. For a while, we shared a bedroom. Then, eventually, we slept in separate rooms. We were maturing, and my mom felt it was best to give us some independence. So, she gave up her bedroom for me.

Despite having separate rooms, I spent most of my time in my brother's room playing with my Barbies and pink dollhouse. "I'm going to play Barbie, and you play Ken," I'd tell Jonathan, passing him the male doll. He'd get bored fast and start playing with his hot wheel's cars or G.I. Joe and Power Rangers action figures. My brother was truly a trooper. To spend quality time with him was the highlight of these years. It didn't matter if we were playing with our toys or on his *Teenage Mutant Ninja Turtle* console, we simply loved being in each other's company.

For a brief amount of time, my uncles Luke and Rick took turns living with us. Their bedroom was in the empty attic. I barely saw Uncle Luke when he lived at our townhouse, but I remember walking up the stairs one afternoon and hearing Uncle Rick blast his favourite Out-Kast tune. *"Hey Ya! Hey Ya!"* he screamed over the speakers in the main washroom.

Our bond was much tighter with our aunts. Felicia, the younger, bubbly, playful aunt, was closer to Jonathan. They shared the same love of being carefree and making people laugh. While I remained close to Celeste, the older, reticent, studious type like me. She continued to be the one person, outside of my mom, with whom I felt the most relaxed around.

Occasionally, Auntie Felicia would take us out with her Trinidadian boyfriend, Donte. We'd cruise around the town in her white Ford Fusion while listening to the newest hip-hop and R&B music on her burnt CD's. In my brother and I's eyes, Aunt Felicia was the coolest.

Because Auntie Celeste was obtaining her undergraduate degree and then attending medical school in Montréal, we didn't see her often. But when she visited us, she continued to assist Mommy. The extra help was always appreciated by us.

When she met her now husband, Eric, they would come bearing gifts during each visit. "Hi, my name is Eric," he told us the first time we met him. My brother took off his shirt. "Look at my muscles!" he roared, pointing at them.

I had a much different reaction to him. I watched Eric's every move while I stood beside Mommy. Only when I sensed he seemed like a good guy did I step outside of my reserved shell, open my mouth to say hello, and thank him for the present he had bought for me and my brother.

If we couldn't see our aunts, whenever they'd travel, we would receive postcards from them. "Mom, did we get any mail from Auntie Celeste or Felicia?" we'd ask her.

"No, there's nothing today, guys."

"*Aw*," we'd say in unison. The thought of receiving postcards from our aunts would make us jump out of our dining room seats. It reminded us that we were dearly loved by them.

Jonathan and I still have a couple of the postcards Auntie Felicia sent us from some of her voyages. Looking at the cards, at this age, brings a smile to my face.

* * *

Alexandru Micu asks in their December 22nd, 2022, article in ZME Science "what's your earliest memory? Statistically speaking, it's likely from when you were two and a half years old, according to a new study." Other studies go even further and suggest there's a possibility we recall explicit memories involving negative emotions more than positive experiences. It might be a survival mechanism used to assist us from enduring similar injurious experiences in the future.

But it's just as important to remember the heartwarming childhood memories that stand out to you. The ones that make you beam with joy as you reminisce. The ones that make your belly hurt from laughter. The ones that evoke happy tears and emotions within you.

As hard as it is to not focus on the bad times, when you allow your inner child to breathe, it will pop up every now and then to remind you of the sweet days. I find comfort in these loving memories that still remind me, and now hopefully you, it's good to remember the *positive* too.

In the early 2000s, here I am, walking and posing with Mommy and Jonathan in our neighbourhood in Aurora, Ontario.

Jonathan and I at our first photoshoot together.

Sitting in the living room with my brother in our townhouse in Aurora during the summertime.

Three-year-old me
posing for the camera.

Three

MAMA WOUND

Corporal punishment is as humiliating for him who gives it as for him who receives it; it is ineffective besides. Neither shame nor physical pain have any other effect than a hardening [of a person]....

— Ellen Key

On a warm July evening in Aurora, I bashfully asked Mom for permission to go outdoors. I could see my neighbours having a blast through the front door glass window, and I wanted to join in on the fun, too. "You can go outside for twenty minutes," Mommy agreed. I was ecstatic!

My friend's black and white bicycle was lying in our front yard. When we approached each other, I asked, "Can I ride your bike?"

"Of course," she said.

The warm breeze riffled through my braided hair. As I pedalled up and down the sidewalk, I took in the fresh scent from the tall pine trees and flowers in my neighbours' gardens. Then I saw people crowding around my front porch. *What are they doing?* I wondered.

To draw attention to myself, I thought it would be cool to playfully shoo them away. "Get off my property!" I shouted, riding past the sea of people. One of those people just so happened to be my best friend's mother, Anita.

"Jamilla, come here," she said, beckoning her left hand. I gently placed the bicycle on the pavement and dashed towards her. "Are you allowed to use such language?"

I froze. "I … I don't know what you're talking about."

"*Are you sure?*" she continued.

"Yes," I said, nodding.

Weeks later, my brother and I spotted Katie and her mother standing on their front lawn. We begged Mom to let us go outside and chat with them. Mommy caved in and followed us.

"Hi, Katie!" I ran towards her. We formed a mini circle, and our mothers talked about grown-up things.

"Why don't you guys go play?" Anita suggested.

"Yeah," Mom said. "Go play!"

That's weird. Why don't they want to talk in front of us? The incident from a couple weeks back flashed into my mind, but I told myself there was no need to panic. I hadn't done anything wrong.

Later that evening, after I had prepared myself for bed, Mom cornered me in the laundry room. "What happened a few weeks ago?"

I stared at her, confused.

"I heard that you swore," she said.

"No, I didn't." I had no idea what swearing was.

"Anita told me you did," Mom replied. And that was all the proof she needed.

As Mommy drew closer, I backed away. "I *didn't* swear," I repeated, crying. My words held no value.

Next thing I knew, I was lying face down on my bed, wailing into my pillow. I was so hysterical that I punched it.

I'll never treat my children this way! I said to myself. *I'll never lay a hand on them!*

* * *

Mom picked up an envelope from our nightstand. "I'll pay it next week," she said. But her eyes looked unsure. I could tell she was trying to decide what to do.

"Why don't you pay it now, Mommy?" I suggested, impulsively. It made more sense to get it over and done with. Delaying the payment was only going to make her worry more.

My words backfired on me. At nine years old, I'd broken the number-one rule in a Black household: *Don't speak your mind.*

"I'm going to spank you," my mom replied. "Pull down your pants!"

Reluctantly, I slid down my go-to light blue jeans. *Don't cry,* I told myself. *Be still. You'll be fine.*

I slowly turned my body so that my backside was facing my mom. From the corner of my eye, I saw her right hand raise. *Whack!*

My legs buckled under the force of my mom's hand. Immediately, I wanted to find a place to hide. I crawled into the closet, curled into a ball, and cried.

As I wept my pain away, I got mad at myself. I'd given in to my emotions, and that made me feel weak. *Why couldn't you be strong?* I asked myself, pounding on my chest.

It took me thirty minutes to calm down. My hands shook as I creaked open the closet door. I resorted to my bed and quietly watched the show my mom turned on the television. Then I went on about my day because, in Black households, whenever you get physically punished, you're forced to act like nothing happened, even though, subconsciously, you never truly forget.

* * *

As teenagers, my brother and I often hung out with our classmates and neighbourhood friends after school. My brother was the biggest goofball. Every once and a while, he'd pull down his pants to show off his butt crack. He knew it would make our friends laugh. But I found his behaviour embarrassing. I didn't like it at all.

"Don't do that, Jonathan!" I'd tell him.

He didn't listen.

One day, after Mom came home from work, all three of us gathered in the kitchen and started conversing. "I saw you pull down your pants," my mom told my brother.

"Yeah," Jonathan said, laughing.

He left to play soccer with his friends, while I stayed inside, trying to complete a project. My goal was to finish it early so I could relax at night. As I worked at the kitchen table, I saw Mommy approaching me from my peripheral view. I tilted my head to face her. *Whack!*

Flabbergasted, I placed my hand on my throbbing cheek. No part of me had anticipated that slap, especially not at that moment or at my age. I was sixteen. I wasn't a child anymore!

A wave of anger rose within me and consumed my mind. I thought about physically fighting my mom back but quickly shook off my thoughts. *Don't do it. Calm down.* My ego wasn't going to get the best of me.

"You were supposed to watch him!" Mom hollered.

I couldn't utter a word. Hot tears flowed down my cheeks. With my blood boiling, I left our apartment.

Outside, I looked for a secluded place in the parking lot to calm my mind. I sat down on the curb and started plotting. I resolved to move out as soon as I could. *And never return again!*

I promised myself that life wouldn't always be like this. I'd make sure of it.

When I returned home, I didn't know what to expect, but I had to face whatever was going to come at me next.

"Oh, Milla, can you grab the bag from the table and give it to me?" Mom asked.

I stood still, annoyed and confused. *Really?!*

In my teenage mind, I couldn't comprehend how my mom could inflict pain on me and then carry on as if nothing had happened. But I didn't want more problems. So, I chose to be the bigger person and "forget" about it.

I breathed in deeply. "Sure, Mom." All I wanted was peace.

For some, as children, we choose the strife-free route. It's the easier way out of the conflict-filled zone because too many things are working against us. The biggest one is physical. We can't win a fight with our parents. We're in an unfair position of inferiority.

In these moments, I felt overpowered by my mother. Belittled. Weak. Hopeless. I felt negatively about myself.

Fix your face! Do you want something else to cry about? Those words were a cue to many of us to not show our feelings. Consequently, we *feared* showing our feelings. We learned to suppress them, both inwardly and outwardly. We internalized the belief that there is no use in reacting to our grief. Our pain.

But there is.

We're human. So naturally, we want to cry when we're hurt, emotionally or physically. Tears soothe our pain.

I always cried. That wasn't a choice for me due to my highly sensitive nature. But what I learned was to silence my voice. Jamilla, the reticent girl, retreated further into her shell after each whack.

I rarely shared my opinions with my mom and relatives unless I was asked to or raised my hand to answer questions at elementary school, even when I wanted to. In fact, I disliked it when my teachers called on me to share my thoughts. I preferred to keep them to myself.

My best friend, Dean, would tease me. "You barely smile. Why are you serious all the time?"

I was thrown off guard when he'd point out my illusory armour, the protective suit I had placed firmly over my heart. "I don't know … Sometimes, I do smile."

The truth is, I found it easier to be straight-faced and mute. That's the only way I could safeguard the beautiful, sensitive, vulnerable girl that existed within me. The "stronger" part of me wanted to protect her. So, the word *impassive* became one of my best-known attributes.

Mommy and I.

Four

CONFINED

I've learned that people will forget what you said, people will forget what you did, but people will never forget how you made them feel.

— Maya Angelou

"**G**randma's going to live with us for a couple of weeks," Mom announced. After suddenly selling her place in Vaughan in 2006, my grandma needed somewhere to stay until construction for a new house was complete. "Okay, Mommy," I answered, eating Kraft dinner.

On the day my grandma was to arrive, Mom glanced at the microwave clock in the kitchen. "Grandma will be here in thirty minutes. Change into nice clothes," she told us.

Jonathan and I watched for her from the front window.

"There she is!" I yelled. We ran to the door. "Welcome, Grandma!"

"Hello!" she exclaimed.

"I'll take your big suitcase upstairs," I told her, grabbing onto the purple handle.

"Thank you, bébé."

Living with my grandma reminded me of the old days. She would pick Jonathan and me up after school, and our custom would continue. If we weren't taking trips to get a treat or stopping by a new eatery, we'd arrive at our front doorsteps around 2:30 p.m. Grandma would plop her butt on the couch and watch *The Young and the Restless*. I'd watch TV with her. Or I'd play the board game *Guess Who?* with my brother.

One evening, after playing a couple of rounds, Jonathan announced that he was bored. He sprinted upstairs to his bedroom.

While I packed up the pieces of the game one by one, I could feel Grandma's ebony eyes on me. I forced a smile, but she could tell I was wearing a mask.

"Can you teach me how to play?" she asked, kneeling down.

"Of course, Grandma!" She got the hang of it really fast. So much so, we played *Guess Who?* together many times after that.

At night, Grandma and I slept on my queen-sized bed together. I didn't mind sharing my bedroom with her. More alone time with my grandmother was a bonus in my eyes. I could receive the attention I secretly yearned for, even though I pretended that I didn't need it.

"Thank you for being kind enough to share your bed," my grandmother told me one day before we shut our eyes. I turned my head towards her. *"You're welcome, Grandma."* And we dozed off.

* * *

When Christmas came around that year, it wasn't how it had been in the past. There were very few presents under the tree. Even so, I didn't ask my mom for an explanation or pout.

Mom looked back and forth at us kids. "We're moving next month," she said. "That's why there's not as many presents. Our new home is the Christmas gift."

My grandmother chimed in. "Yes, a house is very expensive."

There was silence in the living room. *Move? Why?* I didn't want to move away from my friends.

* * *

Months before this day, Grandma had been trying to persuade one of her children to go in on the mortgage. I realize now, upon reflecting on it, that my grandmother, a widow and single mother, was struggling to stay afloat. She needed financial support from her three young adult children (Auntie Celeste, and my uncles Luke and Rick were living at the home in Vaughan), whom she did everything for, but who she also felt were taking advantage of her by not contributing to the household expenses. Uprooting, to her, symbolized a fresh start. Knowing this now, I'm unsure how moving was going to resolve my grandmother's issue of feeling burdened by her children.

My uncle Luke called my mom after he and the other siblings declined to be on the mortgage with my grandma. "Moving to Caledon will be a great opportunity for you. You'll be a first-time homebuyer," he said.

In the future, when Mom could afford her own home, she would benefit from a percentage of the equity she had built. Mom also reasoned that Caledon was closer to the Greater Toronto Area, providing her with a broader selection of job opportunities. Besides, she felt we had outgrown Aurora. It was time for a change.

"I'll sign the mortgage with you," Mom told my grandma.

"Parfait," she responded.

At work, my mom let her manager Steven know she was going to resign. "I'm moving in with my mother," she told him and some of her coworkers.

"Are you *sure* this is really what you want to do?" they asked her.

Each time, my mom told them the same thing with pure intent in her voice. "Yes, we're a tight knit family. It's my mother."

Those questions were asked for two reasons: my mother's coworkers wanted her to be certain about mixing family and business together. From their experiences, things went sour when family and money were involved.

And they also wondered if she was prepared to live with her mother again. As they saw it, my mom was sacrificing a lot. She was giving up her freedom and quitting her new, decent-paying job at Wells Fargo.

"Be careful, Sandra," they warned her. "Think about this."

* * *

"Will you miss me when I move?" I asked Kai, Dean, and Paige during recess.

"Yes," they replied.

My chest felt heavy. Life was going to go on, and someday my best friends and I were going to forget about each other. When I said my farewells to them at the end of the school day, my eyes moistened. *Stop!* I told myself. Showing emotions in front of people made me feel unshielded. So, I fought back my tears and lifted my head up high. *Beauty lies ahead.* There was no need to sulk.

Back at our complex, my brother and I waited in the meeting room until Mom came home from work. Paul, a curly haired man, kept an eye on us as he loaded our boxes into a white rental truck.

Within an hour, Mommy arrived and called a taxi to take us to our new residence at 720 Ambers Avenue. As we approached, I craned my neck to get a better view of the house. "Wow, it's huge!" The idea that this was going to be my home thrilled me.

Grandma opened the chestnut front door. From the sidewalk, I caught a glimpse of the interior of the house. I wanted to run inside and gallivant around.

"Take off your boots," my grandma instructed us, pointing at the light grey outdoor mat on the ground.

She led us upstairs where the bedrooms were located. I looked around big-eyed. There was so much open space.

That wasn't something I was used to having in Aurora.

"This is my room!" I exclaimed as Jonathan and I ran around and giggled. The room was spacious enough to fit the whole family. I didn't know bedrooms like that existed!

Grandma wasted no time showing us the actual bedroom Jonathan and I would share. Mom's room was next to ours. The odd thing was, there were enough rooms for each of us, four to be exact. The remaining bedroom, Grandma informed us, was for Uncle Luke.

My mom had been under the impression that the house was for the four of us. That was the whole point of us moving together. For all of us to have our own space.

Grandma gave us a brief tour of the first floor. Within seconds, we found out she had compartmentalized where our crockery and cutlery would go: in two or three wooden cabinets. For groceries, we were assigned a couple of shelves in the fridge and freezer. We would be required to buy our groceries separately. Hers were for *herself* only.

From that day on, if I wanted to eat something she purchased, I'd ask her for permission. If I wanted to be bold and sneak something, I had to be meticulous about it. I'd slip a Haagen-Dazs ice cream bar underneath my shirt or conceal green grapes in my cupped hands.

To avoid unpleasantries, Mom thought it would be best to stay out of Grandma's way. My mom would make dinner as soon as we got home. We ate quickly at the glass dining room table. "Hurry guys, your grandma is almost home," Mommy would say. Then we'd wash our plates, put them in the dishwasher, and stay in our room for the rest of the day.

And Mom was mindful about the smell of the meals.

"Ça sent mauvais!" my grandma said, sniffing the kitchen after arriving home from work one day.

"Sorry, Mom," my mother replied. "I cooked liver. It's

good for my health." My mom would never make a dish with liver at 720 Ambers Avenue again.

Late one evening, I decided to grab a snack. I'd eaten hours ago and had the munchies. "Don't go," Mom pleaded.

I tip-toed towards the unlit kitchen.

What are you doing here?" Grandma said.

My heart beat out of my chest. "I'm getting a snack," I answered.

"Well, you shouldn't be downstairs!"

I searched the fridge. No snacks. So I ran upstairs to my room.

My feelings were hurt. But my grandmother's reaction wasn't surprising. Deep down inside, that's what I expected would happen. I'd just wanted to prove both Mom and me wrong.

* * *

After we settled into the house, Aunt Felicia, then twenty-two years old, started living with us. She cut her two-month Christmas vacation in Trinidad with her boyfriend, Donte, short. A traumatic event had occurred during the trip that left her shaken up. She entered the family home single, heartbroken, and noticeably mute.

"You can take my room for now," Mom told her. My mom moved and shared a queen-sized bed with me, and Jonathan slept in the other bed. But Aunt Felicia's "temporary" stay ended up being permanent, too.

When Felicia and Celeste stopped renting the apartment they shared after briefly moving out of Grandma's house to seek independence, Felicia bought a house in Milton. But she could no longer afford it. So, she began renting out the house and lived with us in Caledon instead.

The bedroom was cramped with three people living in it, but we made the best of our situation. Sharing space is what we were used to. And, weirdly, I didn't like the idea of us being in separate rooms. Even though my mom was close by, she seemed far away.

* * *

At my new school, I was gifted with some semblance of freedom.

My teacher, Miss Texas, a pretty, fair-haired woman with freckles, introduced me to the class. "Everyone, this is Jamilla!" A bunch of eyes stared at me. I stood at the front of the classroom, stiff as a rock, and stared back.

But in no time, I made friends. This school was different. There were so many Black kids. In Aurora, I could count the number of Black faces in my class on one hand. I was overjoyed to see people who looked like me.

I attached myself to a certain crew, mostly boys. We raced each other during recess. I mimicked their ways, walking with a hop in my step and making fun of girly-girls. I thought acting like a boy was cool. The masculine vibe was attractive to me.

In retrospect, that type of energy was something I needed badly. It was almost nonexistent at home, where I was surrounded by strong-willed women. In the presence of guy friends, I felt respected, valued, and protected.

There were times when I'd feel exposed in front of my friends, though. The special day in June—Father's Day—arrived quickly. Ms. Texas gave us instructions at the beginning of class. "Let's start making cards."

I sat on my ash-coloured seat and began sketching birds that looked like an upside-down number three. Ms. Texas walked towards my wooden desk. "Jamilla," she said, getting down on one knee. "Why aren't you making a Father's Day card?"

"I don't have a dad," I replied, grinning.

Her jaw dropped. "*Hmmm,*" she said, biting her lower lip. "I'm sure there's someone else you can make one for?"

I held my head down. "No, there's no one."

I liked Uncle Rick's calm demeanour, so I'd hang out in his room whenever he let me. But he was at university.

"Oh! I could make a card for my uncle Luke," I told Ms. Texas.

"Great!" she answered.

I wrote "Happy Father's Day" in large, colourful letters on green cardboard paper. Ms. Texas was pleased. I was too.

A few mornings later, I gave Uncle Luke the card. He thanked me and pinched my cheek. I hopped away from his room beaming with joy and relief that he didn't reject my gift—or me.

* * *

I had a dream about my father soon after that day. "Dad," I shouted, running towards him in an unfamiliar place. "I found you! At last, we're finally meeting!"

As I hugged him tightly, tears streamed down my face. When I woke up, my eyes were still wet. In my nine years of life, I had never cried over my dad's absence.

But just like the ducts in my eyes had opened the door to let my sorrow flow, my heart had been pounding harder to tell me something: I needed to release the resentment I'd been carrying within me towards my mother. The anger and bitterness were hardening my heart.

I wanted to let the anger go, but it was difficult. I couldn't ask my mother about my father. I couldn't even remember what he looked like anymore! All I kept wondering was, *What was this secrecy all about?*

My brother must have been thinking the same thing. After my dream, he asked Mom about our dad. That afternoon, I not only found out that my father's name was Marcus and that he had named me, but I also discovered something I had been struggling to remember.

Mommy looked at me and chuckled. "People have always said it's funny how I gave birth to a child who looks exactly like him."

I didn't know if that was a good or a bad thing. I was just happy to have another clue.

* * *

Mom learned she was suffering from hypertension before her twenty-ninth birthday. In a matter of months, Mommy began having unmanageable headaches and sporadic nose bleeds. She tried to hide it from us.

Then she couldn't anymore.

"Mom, your nose is bleeding," I said.

"It's okay. I'm fine," she replied from the bed. "Can you grab me a Kleenex?"

I handed Mom a tissue. She wiped her nose and took a nap.

The following week, my mom made a doctor's appointment and found out her diastolic and systolic numbers were high. Mom changed her diet, but it didn't work. The diastolic number didn't go down enough, so the doctor gave her some pills. Watching her adjust to the side effects was devastating. Most of the day, she slept. She barely mustered the strength to cook for us. The effort depleted her.

Seeing this ignited a fear I had of being abandoned. At the age of nine, the thought of losing my mother and being an orphan shook me to the core. *Don't think that way*. Negativity was not doing me any good, so I tried to make the fear go away not just for myself but also for Jonathan. I didn't want him to feel the weight of my worry. He was just a child.

I chanted encouraging words over Mommy. "She's going to be okay," I'd repeat until I believed it. I had to remain positive, make sure Mom got enough rest, and protect my brother's innocence. So, I'd quietly play games with him.

All the while, I felt alone. My grandma, Aunt Felicia, and Uncle Luke, who was hardly home, rarely checked up on us. There was only one time when Auntie Felicia did.

"Sandy, how are you doing?" she asked, carefully cracking our bedroom door open.

"Oh, I'm doing fine," my mom replied, struggling to lift her head.

When I couldn't shove down my feelings any longer, I went downstairs to talk with my grandmother. She was a nurse. There was no way she wouldn't have an answer for me.

"What's wrong with Mom?" I asked her.

"She's just tired," Grandma responded, moving food around in the freezer. "Do you want ice cream?"

"Okay." The ice cream warmed me up.

* * *

During the holidays, family gatherings were hosted at the home in Caledon. Christmas time always had a way of brightening my mood. It seemed to have a similar effect on my grandmother too. She'd decorate the staircase with bow ties and sparkly, translucent ribbons. "I'll decorate the tree with purple and blue ornaments," she told Mommy one year.

Irrespective of the good vibes that typically arise, I'd feel discomfort as soon as everyone gathered around the feast laid out on the kitchen island. Whenever I grabbed smoked fish, red snapper, pondu, red kidney beans, or plantains to put on my plate, I sensed eyes watching me.

I'd see my grandma look at Felicia, and Felicia looking back at her mother. Their mouths would move. Through all their mumbling from across the room, I could never figure out what was being said.

"Okay, that's enough," my mom would tell me. "Leave some food for everyone else."

My plate wouldn't even be half-way filled up. But I understood why Mommy would tell me to stop. There was blatant favouritism within our household. And I felt if something were to happen, my mom would be too afraid to stick up for herself.

I didn't understand why. My mom was the eldest daughter. In a Congolese household, she was customarily viewed as the second mother, and therefore, an authority figure. That title commanded respect. But strangely, we found ourselves walking on eggshells with everyone. It was easier to follow these rules: be obedient, stay quiet, and don't question anything.

* * *

When we moved into that house, it was as if a switch went off overnight with my grandma. I woke up one day and the kind and nurturing woman I knew was gone. In her place was an unapproachable stranger.

Mommy made excuses. "Grandma's tired from work," she would say.

I sensed there was more to it than that. But I was confused. Why wouldn't Grandma like us anymore?

I now understand that we were a nuisance to my grandmother. All she wanted was my mother's financial assistance to acquire *her*, not our, new home. So, we lived in a house where we weren't supposed to exist.

That's no way to live. No child should be made to feel unwanted in the place they call home.

On Earth and beyond, the *feeling* from experiences we have with other human beings is what we're left with. These experiences shape a person and, even deeper, their soul forever in a positive or negative way. The feeling of anxiety and toxicity from this period in my life is what I have sadly never forgotten. It has stuck with me ever since.

Mommy, Jonathan, and I during our second-to-last
Christmas in Aurora.

Five

UNNOTICED

*Never let a stumble in the road be the end of the
journey.*

— Unknown

$\mathcal{S}$andy, do you and the kids want waffles?" Auntie Felicia asked, opening our bedroom door. We all said yes.

My brother and Auntie Felicia went downstairs. I followed, soundlessly, and hid behind a half wall. Aunt Felicia, all dressed in taupe, beat the batter and joked with my brother. When the waffles were ready, she grabbed tongs and set two aside on a white plate for Jonathan. They sat together at the dining room table, and like she often did, Auntie Felicia tickled him.

I continued to stand in the hallway, too shy to interrupt. After a while, I peeked over the wall at the large kitchen island. There were no more Belgian waffles.

Aunt Felicia spotted me. I turned around and hid again.

I struggled to build up the courage to ask for a waffle. All my aunt Felicia was going to do was rattle my nervous system. But eventually I got tired of waiting and entered the kitchen.

"Well, do you want a waffle?" she snapped.

"Yes," I replied, my voice shaky. A bubbling sensation arose in the lower part of my stomach. It bubbled up so high that I ran up the oak staircase and burst into tears before I got to my bedroom.

What I didn't know was Aunt Celeste, who had been visiting us at the family home, was there, listening to our interaction. When I returned to the kitchen, she came to my aid.

"She reacted that way because you yelled at her," Celeste told Felicia with a stern look on her face. "It's unkind to make something for one child and not the other."

That behavioural pattern from Aunt Felicia was all I had ever known. She'd buy a Game Boy for Jonathan, who didn't want one, even though she knew it was on my wish list. Then Grandma would step in and buy one for me too. Auntie Felicia would make mango smoothies or waffles and forget about me, or she would constantly serve me last.

She just didn't like me. I never understood why. Was it something I did or said? Her behaviour towards me didn't make sense.

At that moment, though, I didn't care about her actions. I was simply relieved to have someone like my aunt Celeste speak up for me when I lost my voice. It still chokes me up.

* * *

As much as my grandma would try to mend the wound created by Aunt Felicia, she showed favouritism, too. Whenever I got the chance, I would sneak into my grandmother's master bedroom and swiftly change the photos in the Valentine's Day heart on her dresser. The photo of my brother, dressed in an orange button-up shirt, was always in front. My photo was behind his.

I hoped she would leave my photo in front for a little while, to show me temporary love. But the next time I checked, Jonathan's picture was back in front. And I became invisible again.

After a while, I gave up.

To be seen, I helped around the kitchen instead. Having a sink free of dirty dishes, and a kitchen island free of crumbs and smudges was important to my grandmother.

So, I'd wash and wipe the cutlery and plates, and place them in the drawers and cabinets.

My grandma came home from a tiring day at the hospital on a Saturday afternoon. "Thank you for washing the dishes, Ja-me," she said. "You've been doing them for weeks now."

For my efforts, Grandma took me to the mall. We shopped for a new school outfit. It felt great to be noticed by my grandmother, even if it was only for a short time.

* * *

One cold morning, the thought of suicide pulsed through me. Alone in the kitchen, I questioned why I felt this way. *What's wrong with me?* Placing my left hand on the middle of my chest, I recognized something. A hole in my heart.

At first, I assumed being fatherless was the major cause. It was the logical thing for me to think. Surely, having an absentee parent would create the blues within any child.

Nah, I thought, shrugging my shoulders. *These are the cards that life dealt me. It is what it is.*

Besides, how could I complain when other people were in worse situations? *I'm doing just fine without Dad,* I reassured myself.

I continued to search for answers, and the word *family* came up. I almost felt as if I didn't belong in the family I was born into. As if I was merely *there*.

Who did I relate to? No one. *Who saw me?* No one. The realization that I was unnoticed cut like a knife.

Seeing the undisguised disinterest towards me from the majority of my family over the years had ushered me to this dark place. And the fact that no one saw my unhappiness confirmed to me of how overlooked I was. If anyone cared, they would have noticed. But maybe if I was gone, I would finally be noticed, and possibly even missed.

On impulse, I picked the smallest black knife from the knife block. It wasn't just any knife; it was the household's most frequently used kitchen knife.

Why not kill yourself? I thought, my eyes filling up with tears. *Go on. Slit your wrist.*

I quivered. *No ... I can't.*

Fear of the unknown, death, prevented me from going through with this irreversible act. I couldn't picture what happened next and trembled at the blankness.

You can't do it, I pleaded again with myself. *You have to help people.*

Knowing that I had a specific purpose to fulfil in this lifetime pulled me back from suicidal thoughts. There was no way I could cut my life short. There was much more for me to do.

What do you want when you're older? I asked myself. My response was simple: internal peace and happiness. On that day, I promised myself that I would make sure I fulfilled my ultimate wish. And it's a promise I still intend to keep. I owe it to little me.

* * *

I'm now aware that this was my first experience dealing with depression. I just didn't know it at the time. There was no way I could have. Emotional intelligence and understanding were lacking in myself and the adults around me.

No one talked about their emotions or mental health issues and how they can arise during different phases of life. My distant nature was overlooked, like that of many children. I was labelled as being weird, rude, or disrespectful by the adults around me sometimes. When, in reality, I had underlying issues such as anxiety and occasional depression, which manifested at higher intensities when I felt emotionally, mentally, and physically unsafe, overwhelmed with life, or unwanted.

Had I known, at age nine, that I was going through a tough time mentally, maybe I wouldn't have thought about suicide. But I'm glad that knowing my purpose saved me. And I want all of you to know that you have something unique and special to do and be, too.

If you don't believe that, your existence alone proves that you're here on Earth for a reason. There's only *one* you. You can never be duplicated. We were all purposefully created, and that will always remain true.

Remember: Don't give up! Keep going! A brighter future does await you.

Six

HIDDEN TRUTHS

For the love of money is a root of all kinds of evil....

— 1 Timothy 6:10 (CSB)

"Grandma wants to visit the Congo," Mommy told us. "I think she's home sick."

It had been fourteen years since my grandmother's feet had last touched the rich soil in her home country. All she was left with were sweet memories from the past and occasional phone calls from relatives who were left behind when she, her husband, and five children fled the Democratic Republic of Congo in 1993.

My grandmother, the oldest of eight, remained closest to her brother, Felipé. After Grandma moved to Aurora in 1998, Felipé and my uncle Luke would assist her in selling my deceased grandfather's properties in the Congo whenever she needed the extra money. From my understanding, they sold the houses together and always agreed about it. But something changed.

Grandma soon found out there was nothing to return back home to. The five remaining houses were mysteriously sold in 2006 for over an estimated half a million dollars. My grandma had no clue. She was outraged.

Hearing this revelation upset everyone, including myself. Knowing that we still had relatives who lived in those houses that now found themselves homeless was hurtful. Not only that, my brother and I would never be able to see the beautiful properties Mommy grew up in and told us glorious stories about. "Our backyard was the size of a football field. One side was for the roosters and rabbits. And we played soccer on the other side."

Those houses were also among the last possessions we had of Papa as a family. Growing up, Mom often told us about how much she adored, loved, and missed her father. "He would give the shirt off his back to a complete stranger," she'd say, her eyes tearing up. "He was a kind man." My grandfather was everything to her. And so, he became everything to me. The news of all his homes being sold was heartbreaking. It devastated all three of us.

Years later, when I was grown, I learned there was much more to this story than Grandma simply wanting to visit her family. When my grandmother and Mom were set to close on the new construction house in Caledon, Grandma found out she hadn't been financially informed properly. There was an outstanding closing fee for the property, a large fee my grandma didn't have the money for. Her plan was to sell the remaining houses in the Congo. That's when she discovered the houses in Kinshasa had been sold, and there was no money left.

Grandma reacted by kicking Uncle Luke out of our home. I disagreed with her decision. There was something about sending my uncle Luke out into the icy streets that didn't sit right with me, Mommy, or Jonathan. We had no say though. In those days, the only "side" to take was my grandmother's if we wanted harmony. So, we stayed in our room and said nothing.

A couple weeks later, Uncle Luke stopped by the house to pick up the rest of his belongings from his room. "Hi, Low Low!" I exclaimed. As usual, he pinched my cheeks. Any other time I would have been annoyed, but I was genuinely relieved to see that he looked well.

Uncle Luke took off his shiny black dress shoes. Then he inquired about my grandmother's whereabouts. "She's in the kitchen," I answered, pointing.

He straightened his shoulders and went in. "Maman, I want to speak with you."

I could sense his nervousness. I felt the same uneasiness within my grandmother too.

They sat at the dining room table, and I slipped to my favourite spot: the third step of the oak staircase. There were no raised voices. My grandmother seemed receptive to what my uncle Luke had to say. It sounded like they were making up.

Suddenly, Auntie Felicia opened her bedroom door. As she thumped down the stairs, my heart pounded faster in my chest. Auntie Felicia stormed into the kitchen, wrapped her right arm around her mother's shoulder and said, "Luke, you did this … You did that to your own mother." Uncle Luke didn't respond.

"Well, Felicia," my grandmother said, stroking her hand. Grandma was trying to reason with Felicia before things escalated. But my grandma was being overpowered by her too.

Aunt Felicia got all in Uncle Luke's face, berating him. He got up from his seat and stood by the backyard sliding door, hoping he would be left alone.

Felicia followed her brother and fired more words at him.

"Maman!" Uncle Luke muttered.

Grandma was mute.

"Felicia, that's enough!" Uncle Luke said repeatedly. "Felicia, move! Move!" He shifted from side to side, but she blocked his way. "Girl, if you don't *move*!"

To diffuse the situation, Uncle Luke bolted for the front door. But Auntie Felicia chased after him.

From the front doorsteps, Felicia taunted Uncle Luke as he ran towards the black car his girlfriend was waiting for him in. "Hey, Luke! Luke!"

Uncle Luke jumped in the vehicle but changed his mind and marched up the front steps of the house. Auntie Felicia stepped outside and closed the door behind her.

I skipped to the front window. They were standing a meter apart, arguing. After a few minutes, Uncle Luke returned to his vehicle and drove off. I then returned to my spot on the staircase.

Auntie Felicia came inside, smirking.

"He hit me across the face!" she hollered, holding her untouched cheek as she jetted towards the kitchen.

My jaw dropped.

My mother had joined Grandma, who was rearranging bamboo baskets containing pop and water bottles, in the kitchen. They exchanged a look. I could tell they didn't believe Auntie Felicia. They hadn't heard a thing.

The whole time, my uncle Rick was in his room. He had returned home to take a few weeks' break away from university in Detroit.

Grandma knocked on his bedroom door and told him what happened. Uncle Rick came downstairs, kissing his teeth. He didn't want any part of the fight between his oldest brother and closest sister, but he was the new man of the house. It didn't matter that he was the youngest child or that he was still in school. He had no choice but to fill in his brother's place now.

Felicia sat on the yellow Italian leather couch and told her story about how her brother "hit" her. Uncle Rick and my grandmother took turns consoling her. "Shhh … everything's going to be okay," they said, rubbing her head and back.

I sat on the adjacent couch. By now, no one was paying any attention to me. *This is so interesting*, I thought. I couldn't fathom why someone would make up such a lie. What was she getting out of it?

Other than having all eyes on her, I had no clue. All I, the nine-year-old child who always paid close attention to details, saw clearly in that moment was that it's *not* good to lie.

In life, however, this old commandment isn't the easiest rule to abide by. The truth is everyone lies. Some fib more than others, and some tell untruths to lesser or greater extents.

The act of lying takes a toll on people though. It affects human beings spiritually, mentally, emotionally, and physically. Dishonesty inhibits us from cleansing ourselves fully because a fib is harder to keep up with than the truth is. Most times, our egos even trick us into believing perpetuating the untruth is better or easier.

But that's untrue. Our brains are forever changed by constant deceit. The negative signals in the amygdala, which regulates our emotions, decrease over time the more we lie. Then our brains eventually become trained to feel less guilt, desensitizing us.

And yet, for whatever reason, we all rarely obey this one fundamental rule.

"We should call the police," Aunt Felicia shouted. "I'm calling the police!"

"It's okay … calm down, Felicia," Uncle Rick said.

"He's outside!"

Through the sliding door, I could see Uncle Luke talking to my mother in the backyard. Maybe he wanted his voice to be heard, too.

"Tell him to leave!" Auntie Felicia cried.

And that's exactly what he did. He was outcast from the family. Never to be heard about or seen until my aunt

Celeste's wedding two years later.

* * *

In the summer of 2008, Aunt Celeste visited the family home during a rare break from medical school. Seeing her at the front door was a pleasant surprise. "Auntie Celeste!" I screamed.

After dinner, Auntie Celeste announced, "Eric and I are planning to purchase a place soon."

"Congratulations!" everyone shouted, clapping.

But, within a few days, my aunt Celeste discovered that she was in debt. Around the time she and her sister Felicia lived in their Milton apartment together, someone had obtained credit cards in her name. She was livid.

Celeste went searching for documents and receipts. She went back and forth between the kitchen and the unfinished basement for an hour.

At first, Mom, Jonathan, and I had no idea what was going on. All we heard from our bedroom was commotion. "Let's go see!" my brother exclaimed as we peaked our heads over the staircase to observe the ruckus on the first floor.

Jonathan and I followed Mom to the kitchen. "What's going on?" my mom asked Grandma.

Grandma took a couple of seconds to respond. "Oh … sit down, Bibi."

Mommy turned on the grey Cuisinart kettle to prepare herself a cup of chamomile tea. While the tea was brewing, we sat down on the dining room chairs at the kitchen table.

My grandmother sat on her favourite spot on the couch and glanced at my mom. "I don't know, Bibi." Then she turned her head and continued watching television.

"Vroom. Vroom. *Vroom*," my brother roared as he drove his Hot Wheels cars on the cabinets.

"You and your brother go somewhere else to play," my mom said.

From the living room, I could barely hear what was being said between my mom and grandmother. So, I had to mind my business. But then, I saw Auntie Celeste enter the kitchen with a ton of documents in her hands.

She briskly grabbed the house phone. "What happened?" my mom asked Celeste.

"Sandy, I believe Felicia did this … I'm calling the bank."

"Celeste, wait," Mommy advised her. "Think about this."

Grandma chimed in too. "Yes, Celeste, think about it."

Celeste phoned. "Hi, my name is Celeste. I'm calling because…." And she headed towards the staircase.

Grandma seemed to be having a breakdown. "Why would such a young, beautiful girl do this?" she asked herself, lowering her hands from up in the air. "I just don't understand."

My grandma scrunched her face as if she were trying to squeeze out tears. But not one drop appeared.

Auntie Celeste went back to the basement and then upstairs again. As I looked upwards from the bottom of the staircase, I saw her standing outside my grandmother's master bedroom, continuing her conversation on the phone.

Upstairs, Felicia screamed "Wait, Celeste!" She must have heard Celeste on the phone.

I tugged on my brother's arm. "Let's go see, Jonathan!"

"No! I don't want to!" he replied sharply.

My brother wanted to stay in the living room where he could play with his Hot Wheels cars on the floor, peacefully. But my intuition kept nagging at me to see what would happen next. So, I ran upstairs.

I perched at the top of the staircase, and watched my aunts chase each other from one bedroom to another. Celeste then went into Grandma's bedroom and closed the door. All I could do was watch them with curiosity in my eyes.

What's the lesson in this? I asked myself.

Jonathan tugged at my sleeve. "Milla, play with me," he begged. He had snuck up behind me, as he so often did.

I grabbed one of his Hot Wheels cars and crashed it into his. But my attention was elsewhere.

The same question resurfaced in my mind. *What's the lesson, Jamilla?* I took in the sight once more and an awareness rushed through my body. *To live within your means.*

I understood that sometimes the lifestyle people portray isn't real. You can live in a big house like ours, buy clothes at the fanciest stores, or purchase whatever you want without thinking twice. But if you can't truly afford it, then you're living a fake life.

Now I also realize that you gain nothing in your internal world when you live to impress the external world. The attachment that people have to possessions keeps them mentally and physically trapped. And while people are on their way to obtain prestige in the outer world, they often don't care about who gets hurt. After all, it's all about what they can gain.

My thoughts were disrupted by a sudden movement. Celeste opened the French doors to their mother's master bedroom. Felicia darted towards her.

Celeste tried to close them again. "No, Celeste!" Felicia hollered as they tussled with the doors. *Bam!*

"Celeste! Celeste! Celeste!" Felicia screamed, banging on the doors.

"Milla, what are they doing?" Jonathan asked.

I could tell my little brother needed comforting from me. "I don't know," I said. "But don't worry about it. Adults are weird."

"Yeah," he agreed. "I hope we won't be like that when we're older."

"We won't," I promised him, chuckling. "We'll be better than them."

After another minute or so, my brother suggested that we go downstairs. He was bored, and there was nothing else for me to gain from seeing them bicker. Their fight was becoming increasingly traumatic for both of us to watch.

We slid down the stairs. *Bump. Bump. Bump.* "I did it faster!" Jonathan yelled.

"Nope, I did!" My brother was always faster. He was the carefree one.

We sat on the green couch in the living room. A door slammed upstairs, and my entire body shook. Auntie Felicia mustn't have gotten anywhere with Celeste. She stayed in her bedroom for *days*.

Mommy was still talking with Grandma in the family room. We waited for about five minutes for a signal from her. It felt like eternity. "C'mon," Mom said, waving us towards her.

Upstairs, the shut doors and silence spoke volumes. For the remainder of the night, we stayed in our room. And for the remainder of her break, Auntie Celeste stayed at her boyfriend's family home.

"Be careful," she warned my mom one day. "If she did this to me, don't think she wouldn't do the same to you."

But Mommy wasn't concerned. She and Aunt Felicia were close.

Seven

BEGINNINGS AND ENDINGS

For nothing is concealed that won't be revealed, and nothing hidden that won't be made known and brought to light.

— Luke 8:17 (CSB)

$\mathcal{B}$*eep. Beep.* "What's that noise?" I asked Jonathan. Seconds later, the honking started up again.

I opened the white Venetian blinds in our living room, and there was Aunt Felicia and Mom sitting in a car. My brother and I ran outside. Auntie Felicia rolled down the driver's seat window.

"This is your new car!" she announced.

"Wow!" we said in unison. "Are you serious?"

"Yes," Mommy answered, nodding. "This is our new car. Hop in. Let's go to Baskin Robbins."

Little did I know, Mom and Auntie Felicia had been thinking about buying a car for a few months. My mom had been taking the transit to work in Mississauga, but her commute was becoming tiresome, and both sisters wanted independence. Buying a vehicle would provide them with that.

But there were two problems: Felicia couldn't purchase a car in her name. Her finances had changed after she spent money on a one-way ticket back to Canada following her break up with Donte during her trip to Trinidad. And despite having renters, she later sold the house she had bought in Milton. Then there was Mom, who only had her G1 licence. Since Auntie Felicia had more driving experience, in the summer of 2007, they decided to buy a vehicle together. The loan was taken out in my mother's name, and Felicia contributed to the down payment.

We carpooled with Auntie Felicia every day. On our way to and from school, we would listen to music she had burnt on plastic CDs. Each one was specifically titled.

One evening, Auntie Felicia popped the R&B disk into the car and started blasting the song, "Diva" by Beyonce. She turned her head as Queen Bey sang the lyrics, "Where yo' boss at?" And then asked my brother and me the same question.

"Mommy!" we replied, pointing at her in the passenger seat. We all burst into laughter.

* * *

The birds' dawn chorus was a lot louder during springtime in 2008. One day, I joked with my mom and Jonathan in our bedroom about being from the UK. All of my favourite singers were either born or lived there, and I wanted to be just like them. Being from the UK seemed cool.

"You were born in England," Mommy admitted.

To say I knew it, would be untrue. I had no idea that my innocent playfulness would help me put colour in one of the many blank spots in my story. I just wanted to be cool too.

Soon after that revelation, Mom received her own news. She was going to get a $3,000 bonus from work, and she couldn't wait to tell Felicia. Mom ran into her sister's bedroom.

"That's nice, Sandy," Felicia replied, pacing.

Mommy came back to our room, deflated. I had a gut feeling that she shouldn't have told her sister.

Weeks later, my mom took my brother and me to the bank. She wanted to open our first savings account. We were getting older, and Mommy wanted to give us a head start on saving for university. She deposited $1,000.

"Thank you, Mommy," I said, hugging her snugly. It was a proud moment for her. For *us*.

* * *

By then, Mommy was sharing the champagne Mazda3 with Auntie Felicia as well as Uncle Rick, who had moved back home permanently after dropping out of university. But neither he nor Aunt Felicia took care of it. Sometimes, they parked it in the driveway with barely any gas in the tank. Without a complaint, Mom would fill it up.

There seemed to be a level of entitlement, and I disliked it. That's why, when Uncle Rick supposedly bumped the rear side of my mom's car in late November 2008, he decided not to tell her. I say *supposedly* because it's still unclear who truly damaged our vehicle.

Auntie Felicia brought it to my mother's attention. "Sandy, the car has a bump!" she said, bursting through our bedroom door.

We ran downstairs. As I struggled to put my pink winter boots on, Mom, Felicia, and Jonathan rushed out.

"Oh my God!" Mommy hollered.

I picked up my pace. "*Wow!*" The dent on the rear end was worse than I thought it would be. It was humongous!

Uncle Rick was out, and Felicia blamed him. My mom was upset. We all were. Not only did Uncle Rick allegedly damage our car, he didn't tell anyone about it.

"I'll talk to him," Mom said. "This is unacceptable!"

Auntie Felicia nodded. "Yeah, it's really not … Let me talk to him tomorrow."

For the next several days, the air in the house felt stiff. No one said a word to each other. Everyone stayed in their rooms.

Meanwhile, my mom discovered that in October and November, Felicia had racked up a hefty toll bill that was collecting interest. Mom asked her about it, and Felicia acted indifferent.

Even as Mom tried to wrap her mind around paying for the toll bill, along with the impending car repairs, she tried to remain understanding with her sister. They continued riding the damaged car to their jobs.

During one of their morning drives, Mom told her sister Felicia that she had gotten her bonus from work. Now, Mommy could relax her shoulders. The bonus would help her pay for the out-of-pocket repair cost. She didn't want to waste more time, so she went to the repair shop.

A week before Christmas, Auntie Felicia came into our bedroom. "Sandy, I want the money for the car down payment back. I'm in a better financial position now, and I'm looking to purchase my own vehicle. You'll need to get your own car insurance."

My mom was taken by surprise. Repaying the down payment wasn't part of their initial agreement.

Neither was it not part of the plan to split the car repair cost. On the day my mom and Felicia picked up the Mazda3 together, they got into an argument. Felicia reneged on her promise to help Mommy pay a portion for the repair. Mom had no money left to pay her remaining bills.

On top of that, my mom was still waiting for Felicia to obtain a letter from their insurance company so that she could get a separate policy. Once again, my aunt Felicia wouldn't cooperate. So Mom called them herself.

"Hi, I need a letter of experience," Mommy said.

"Okay," the service agent responded. "Ma'am … you aren't insured with us."

Mom paused. "What are you talking about?"

When the Mazda3 was purchased, Aunt Felicia called the insurance company to get a policy for her and my mother. Felicia told my mom that they were both insured and that Mom was registered as one of the owners with a G2 license. Now, Mom discovered that for two years, Felicia had been listed as the sole registered owner, and that Felicia hadn't updated my mom's licence information. So Mom hadn't built a proper driving history.

Worse than that, she had been driving uninsured for almost two months. After Felicia told Mommy about her plan to purchase her own vehicle, she abruptly cancelled the policy and took the full premium refund. Mom was furious!

She strode to Grandma's master bedroom. "I need to talk to you," Mom said.

"Okay," Grandma replied, dressed in a black mini skirt and heels. Mom had caught her mother just before she was on her way out of the house.

"Felicia removed me from the insurance policy."

I listened to the conversation from the top of the staircase, hoping Grandma would say the right thing. She said *nothing*. Instead, she looked my mom dead in the face and walked away from her. When she passed me on the stairs, her eyes were void of emotion. I got goose pimples.

A few days later, my grandma sent my mom an email. Although we lived in the same house, my family stopped talking to each other. Email became our main way of communicating. "Leave me out of it," Grandma said. She was putting herself first.

Between getting our car repaired, refunding Felicia for the down payment, buying insurance, and paying the toll bill and her portion of the house bills, Mom's $3000 bonus and paychecks went down the drain. She didn't even have money for groceries. During those two months, Auntie Celeste and friends helped us out.

Financially, my mother had been depleted. And then she was gaslit about monies owed.

Through email, my mom pleaded over and over again to receive something from her sister Felicia. *Anything*. In lieu, Felicia threatened my mom to get a lawyer involved to settle the dispute.

One afternoon, we encountered Felicia in the hallway. While we walked towards our room, we said nothing to her. She looked at us, muttered words, and slammed her bedroom door.

"What did she say?" Mom asked me, her tone filled with aggravation.

"She'll put you in jail."

It would be easy to pretend that Felicia's comment didn't trouble me, then and now, but the reality is that it had. Why would Felicia say that? Why would she treat us this way? The latter is a question I still wrestle with.

"Whatever," Mom responded. She was sick of it! I was too.

* * *

My eyes darted towards the mail sitting on the glass side table in the family room as Mom removed our take-out dinner from paper bags in the kitchen. Grandma had always placed her mail there after everyone in the house had been handed theirs, but that day, the stack of envelopes puzzled me. The pile was unusually high.

"Put that back," Mom said as I skimmed through the mail.

"But Mom, there's mail with your name on it."

"What? Let me see!" She peeled open the envelope and frowned. "Who's Alpine Limited?"

"Huh?" I replied.

"There's a $56,000 loan in my name."

When my mom called Alpine Limited, she found out that five months after she had signed off on the mortgage agreement with her mother, someone took out a $56,000 line of credit against the house. The loan was obtained in my mother and grandmother's names, even though Mommy knew nothing about it. And it was all used up. In one short phone call, my mom discovered that she was in a lot of debt.

Mom sent an email to Grandma. "I won't pay a bill until I get no less than $800 for the car repairs and $300 for the insurance premium."

My mom's refusal to pay the house bills further upset my grandmother. And when she heard from Felicia that my mom had been discussing the loan with friends, she was outraged.

Grandma and Felicia scurried into the master bedroom and eavesdropped on my mom's conversation in our bedroom after we had eaten lunch one day. "What family?" Mom said, chuckling while talking on the phone. "I have *no* family. Family doesn't do this to you!

The following night, Uncle Rick placed a white envelope on our bed and left the room.

"Mom, here's the envelope," I said.

"Put it there," Mommy replied, gesturing at the nightstand. She no longer cared about being reimbursed. She lay face down on her pillow.

Mom completely shut down. It scared me. All I could think was, *Why are they doing this to my mom? Why are they being so mean? She's not feeling well.*

Hindsight allows me to see that, out of the three of them, Uncle Rick was different. Maybe he did care but couldn't show it. As I see it, he was a pawn. Someone who was vulnerable and used as a shield to protect his mother and closest sister from any threat of danger. Be damned if his eldest sister, niece, and nephew got hurt in the crossfire. He had a duty to uphold.

Grandma, as she said, was focusing on herself. It didn't matter if right or wrong was staring her in the face. When Felicia, the daughter with whom she did everything—ate, gossiped, travelled, and shopped—was involved, she always turned a blind eye.

But I'm unsure what Auntie Felicia's motives were. Her life was turned upside down when Donte and she parted ways. She went from being an independent young woman with a house in her name to being a twenty-six-year-old woman who was back to living not only with her mother but also her sister and two children. That wasn't what she had signed up for, I'm sure. Was it her plan to bring everyone down with her, though? Or was she so blinded by trying to maintain the lifestyle she once had that she was unconcerned about how her actions would affect everyone else? These are questions I may never have the answer to or fully understand.

In a matter of weeks, "family" had broken my mom down financially, emotionally, mentally, and physically. Pain was written all over her face. Yet, Grandma was still expecting Mommy to contribute to the mortgage payment and bills. There was *nothing* left to give.

Mom decided we had to leave. She started saving for the first and last months' rent on a new place for us and told Grandma about her plans. "My children and I won't continue living in a toxic environment. I don't want any money from the house. Please remove my name from the deed and mortgage."

* * *

Over the past year, Celeste and Felicia made amends. Aunt Celeste would call the house to catch up and make small talk every now and then. When she became aware of what was going on in the house, Auntie Celeste came to my mother's aid and assisted her with crafting emails to my grandmother and Felicia. "Sandra, say this instead," she'd advise her.

With the help of Auntie Celeste, everyone agreed to cordially discuss the situation. Walking through the front door after our outing with Aunt Celeste made my hands sweat. I didn't know what to expect. A part of me thought that things weren't going to go well. But I tried to remain optimistic.

"Kids, go upstairs," Aunt Celeste told my brother and me.

It didn't take long for things to get heated. My body was quivering. My pulse pounded ultrafast in my neck.

"What's going on?" my brother asked.

"I don't know." I wanted to respect Aunt Celeste's command to stay in our bedroom, but the commotion was unnerving for both of us. "I'll go downstairs. Stay here."

From the bottom step of the staircase, I listened to the argument going on between my mom, grandma, and her siblings in the kitchen. "I don't know how the $56,000 line of credit got on my record," Mommy said.

I slipped towards the kitchen and hid behind a wall. Mom was standing at the far end of the kitchen, beside Celeste.

"I didn't sign for it," she continued. I've never seen the document!"

"Remember where I got you from!" Grandma retorted. She was dressed in a light blue robe and white slippers. Felicia and Rick stood on opposite sides of her.

"I did *not* accumulate that debt!" my mom hollered.

Grandma picked up a glass cup from the kitchen island and threw it across the room. Mommy ducked. The glass hit the ground and shattered.

The look on my mother's face was one of complete disbelief and pure *innocence*. She looked like a child to me.

"Leave it alone!" Celeste pleaded, spreading her arms wide to protect my mother. Mommy couldn't take in what her sister was saying. She shot words right back at her mom.

"Shut up!" Uncle Rick shouted, lunging towards my mom. "Why don't you just shut up!"

Just then, my brother reached his soft hand out to me. He'd silently made his way downstairs and had seen Uncle Rick's aggression. I grabbed his hand. He squeezed tight and laid his head on my shoulder. We stood motionless and watched the fight.

All I felt was pain and guilt. Pain because there are certain things in life that touch your soul in an *unspeakable* way. And guilt because I couldn't help my mom defend herself. Nor could I protect my brother from seeing our mom being attacked.

What I know rationally is it wasn't my job to protect my mother. I was only a child. And yet, to this day, what I feel in my twenty-six-year-old body is guilt.

Felicia turned her head and noticed we were standing right there. She sneered at us and didn't say a word. Seeing us meant *nothing* to her. If anything, it fueled her verbal attacks on my mom.

From the look on her face, I could tell the fight wasn't going to end well or anytime soon. Tears trickled down my cheeks. I didn't know what to do.

The one thing I did know was that I didn't want my brother to watch the fight anymore. "Go back upstairs," I told him. "Okay," he said, running up the stairs in his green pyjamas.

I paused at the bottom of the staircase. *What can I do? Think! Think!* As I pondered, Felicia approached me with her arms crossed and told me to go upstairs. Any other time, I would have complied.

"No," I said.

She walked away as if in shock. And I proceeded to think. *Get the phone!* I ran to our bedroom, grabbed my mother's cell phone, and recorded the remainder of the altercation. We would have proof if we needed it in the future.

Afterwards, my brother and I sat on our beds in silence, waiting for Mom. I swear God must've heard our internal cries. Two minutes went by, and she was walking through our door.

"Hi, Mommy, are you okay?" I asked her.

She responded like any mother would, "Oh, yes." We talked and laughed about lighter things for the rest of the night.

A couple days later, I wrote a letter to my relatives in spite of my mom's apprehension. I had to say something. "Be respectful," Mom told me. I was.

No one replied.

From: jamilla kabongo
Date: January 16, 2010 at 9:13:28 AM EST
To: The Kabongo Family

Hello,
Everyone this is Jamilla! <u>Just in case some are thinking Mom had something to do with this e-mail, she did not; these are my judgements, and my opinions!</u>

First of all, I think this matter of sitution that is going on in this household is very heartbreaking in my perspective. Jonathan and I are forced to hear and see all of these family disputes carry on year by year and I'm truely and honestly heartbroken and disgusted by all these situations that carry on. I am saddened by all of this and wish that this family argument can be resolved in an adult like way, so me and Jonathan won't have to live in an environment where <u>family</u> is always fighting.

I am very hurt about what some people have said and happy about what others have said and been able to see the light of day and to be strong enough and brave enough to tell the truth. (Mom and Auntie Celeste)

(1) I am not being poisined by anyone, I am not a little girl anymore and I am old enough to make my own judgements and opinons.

Gramma: **Really all mom wants from you and only wants is for you to take her off your house (mortgage). Please stop talking about the money and money because she does not care about the money from you. My love for you will never change no matter what happens, but I was truly heartbroken when you couldn't come upstairs to see if your own grandchildern were okay the night of the fight.**

Felicia: I am truley **devasted** and **sad** to see you in what again (**a fight**). You have been in **every fight** and its disgusting.... I HATED THE PART OF THE FIGHT WHERE YOU LOOKED DIRECTLY AT ME AND JONATHAN AND YOU CONTINED TO TRY TO POTENEIAL FIGHT MOM....

Rick: I love you no matter, but I am **devasted** that you and grandma can't see the truth and an 11 year old can. **No one told you all to pick side that's your own opinons.** I didn'tlike the choice of words you used towards my mom. Yes mom has been yelling a lot, but in frustration of what your ... sister Felicia.... No she has not been slamming doors, that's been Felicia. Thank-you for thinking of us all the time though.

Auntie Celeste: Celeste I WILL ALWAYS LOVE YOU!!!!!! THANK- YOU FOR SUPPORTING AND HELPING MOM IN THESE DIFFICULT SITUATIONS ... I WILL ALWAYS LOVE YOU NO MATTER WAHT!!

Mommy: I am truley proud of you for sticking up for yourself and not letting people take advantage of you anymore. I hope you stick on that role because no matter how much of a good person you are, you will always be stabbed in the back!!!!!!!!!!! (remember that). Fight for what you belive in and feel and GOD WILL ALWAYS BE ON YOUR SIDE!!!!!!!! I LOVE YOU!!!!!!!!!!!!!!!!!!!!!!!!!!!!!!!

Now for some of you, you probably won't care and others you will. Thank you for taking the time to read what Jonathan and I have to say. Remember you always need to forgive but God knows some won't forget!!!!!

Sincerly, Jamilla

TRANSITIONS

There's a lesson hidden in everything. You just have to find it.

— Unknown

$\mathcal{S}$hortly before my twelfth birthday, my classmates and I were talking outside during recess. Neil had been away yesterday. "I wasn't feeling well," he said. "My mom let me stay home from school." Everybody thought that was the coolest thing ever.

I wondered what it would be like to have the house to myself. My brother and I weren't allowed in the house unless our mother was there. But it was nice to imagine being alone at home.

One morning, I didn't want to go to school. Mentally, I wasn't there.

I reached deep into my diaphragm for a faint pitch. "Mommy, I'm not feeling well. Can I stay home?"

My mom placed her right hand on my forehead. No fever. "You still have twenty minutes before I drop you off at school. Rest. Then see how you feel."

I lay in bed, conflicted. I didn't want to create more problems for my mother. *Just go to school, Jamilla,* I told myself. But I wasn't in the mood to go.

"How are you feeling?" Mommy asked me again.

"I still don't feel good," I lied.

Mom placed her right hand on my forehead one last time and told me I could stay home. "Be quiet though. And *don't* go downstairs."

I was soon bored. I had to be soundless. That meant no television. Nothing.

All I could do was entertain my thoughts and listen to my stomach rumble. I hadn't had breakfast. At noon, I gave myself a pep talk. *You're almost there.* Mom would be home at 4 p.m.

At 3 p.m., I caved in. When I got to the bottom of the staircase, Grandma spotted me. She was sitting on the yellow Italian leather couch, watching television.

"You're here?!" She grimaced.

"Yeah, I wasn't feeling well."

She had no response. I opened the fridge, but there was nothing to eat. So I went back to my room.

The second I heard the front door open, I hurried downstairs and greeted Mommy and Jonathan. "Hi!" we shouted, hugging each other. They took their winter gear off. Mom put our KFC dinner on the countertop, and we fled to our bedroom.

"Mom, Grandma knew I was here," I confessed, feeling guilty.

"Oh, who cares," she replied.

I was relieved. I thought I'd be reprimanded for disobeying. But I sensed it wasn't over. Mom still had to go downstairs to get our dinner.

"I'm going to take a shower," I said.

"Okay, we're going to grab the KFC from downstairs," Mommy replied.

Within minutes I heard loud shouting. I turned the shower faucet off, wrapped a towel around my body and stepped into the hallway. Auntie Felicia's door was wide open. Her being downstairs made my heartbeat quicken. I sprinted to the main floor.

My mother and brother were holding hands. They were backing away from the taunts of my grandmother and Aunt Felicia, who were sitting on the leather couch.

"Stop it," Grandma said, stroking Felicia's arm with

a grin on her face. "She can't handle stress … She has high blood pressure."

"What high blood pressure?" Felicia said. "She caused it herself!"

Mommy and Jonathan headed up the stairs. Felicia jumped up and charged after them.

I stayed in the living room, waiting for an opportunity to be with my mother and brother. Upstairs, Felicia shouted, "Remember how it felt where you were! Remember who saved you!"

My eyebrow raised. *What is Felicia talking about?*

Once I heard, *Bam!* my attention was no longer on her odd comments. I thought Mom and Jonathan were safely in our bedroom. But when I got to the top of the staircase, I saw our bedroom door open and Felicia's closed. I bolted into our adjacent bathroom and saw Auntie Felicia's mouth moving. Mom got fed up and darted towards her.

"Mom, stop! Stop!" My brother tried to hold her back.

Pee streamed down my legs. When I snapped out of my state of shock, I entered the washroom and helped my brother pull our mother back.

Felicia chuckled, slammed the adjoining bathroom door on my mom's face and ran downstairs.

I closed our bedroom door. "What happened?" I asked them.

Mommy didn't answer. She was fuming. And Jonathan had a frightened, dazed look on his face.

I went into the bathroom to clean up and change my clothes. Then I heard Mom's voice. "The police are here." I yanked my blue jeans on and unlocked the bathroom door.

"Really?"

"Yes!" Mom replied.

We went into Uncle Rick's empty bedroom and looked out the window. Sure enough, a police car was parked in our driveway. Given Aunt Felicia's previous threat about putting my mother in jail, this didn't seem random. Someone in the house must have called them.

Mommy opened the front door and greeted the officer.

The police officer looked us up and down. "I got a call about a disturbance."

My hands were trembling. I didn't want her to think we were the problem.

"There's nothing going on," Mom assured her.

Grandma intervened. "She left her sick daughter at home alone."

Police officer Sharon was unfazed. Before Grandma inserted herself between them, Sharon and my mom were talking about being mothers, and my age. "Yeah, that's legal. She's almost twelve years old. I'm a single mother. I do that all the time with my daughter."

"And the boy … He's always playing basketball outside," Grandma said. That wasn't true. We rarely played in the backyard. Whenever we did, it was a problem.

The officer's mouth dropped. She ignored my grandmother and directed the conversation to my mother.

Grandma walked away but came back. "Tu es stupide! Tu es stupide!" she shouted.

Mom shot back, "I'm stupid?"

Living with my mother, I had an insight into her ways: her temperament, her mannerisms, what ticked her off. I knew her better than anyone. Within that five-foot-three-inch body, a feisty woman existed. But she'd only appear in full force when pushed to her limits.

At this moment, she had emerged. I had been waiting for that feistiness to take over her. When it did, I was *so* proud of Mommy for standing up for herself and giving her voice life.

Grandma was speechless. Her first-born daughter's retort must have struck a nerve in her. She went away without a peep.

"Look, I'm not sure what's going on here," Officer Sharon said. "I'm going to go. But no more disturbances."

The three of us bowed our heads. "Okay."

We returned to our bedroom and waited about three hours before venturing to the kitchen to fetch our, now cold, KFC dinner. While Jonathan and I ate, Mom talked on the phone with our friend's mother.

"Sandra, I think it might be best if you leave the house," Daisy said.

"Oh no, I'm sure we'll be fine," Mom replied.

Felicia called the police to complain about "loud talking." Before we knew it, we were back downstairs talking with the same officer. She knew we weren't the problem, and she beckoned us outside to talk privately with her.

"Mommy wasn't talking loudly," I told her. During the past months, my mom's tone on the phone had occasionally been louder than usual. But that night, she spoke calmly with Daisy.

"I know," she said. "It's obvious to me that something isn't right with your grandmother and aunt. When she talked about the kid playing basketball, I thought 'Wow! That's a *child*!'"

We talked for about fifteen minutes. Then she told us, "Look, I don't know what's going on, but this is the second call I've gotten at this address. My boss is going to start asking me questions. I know it's not you guys, but I think it's best you leave."

The police officer wanted us to be okay. She was rooting for us.

Back inside, my mom called Daisy. "I might need to take you up on your offer."

Daisy was understanding, considering it was almost midnight. We packed as many clothes and items into our backpacks and small bags as we could fit. Aunt Felicia came downstairs, smirking, and closed the dark brown door behind us.

"Wow!" I said, as I climbed into the backseat.

"I know," Mommy replied. "We gotta go."

We stayed in the guest room. Our friends did their best to make us feel at home, but for the most part, Mom, Jonathan, and I kept to ourselves, watching late night talk shows, talking, and laughing. We needed alone time to breathe. All we wanted was rest and peace.

Every day after work, my mom gave Daisy a courtesy phone call to ensure it was okay for us to come over. One day, Daisy didn't answer. Mommy tried again. "Maybe they're not home," she said.

"Let's check their house," I suggested.

We drove by and saw them. Our calls were being ignored. We weren't mad at them. We were grateful that they'd taken us in for a couple of days.

"What are we going to do?" I asked Mommy, holding back tears. Inside, I was breaking down, fast. But I couldn't let myself cry. I had to be strong for Jonathan and Mommy.

"I don't know," she replied. "I've looked up homeless shelters. I'll call one of them."

"Okay," I said. I concentrated on the harmonious gospel songs from the iWorship II album playing in the background. They kept me from sobbing.

A couple minutes later, Mommy thought of calling Auntie Celeste. "It's late. But let's see if she'll answer."

One ring went by. Then two. And three. On the third ring, she picked up the phone.

"Hi Celeste. The kids and I have nowhere to go. It's the middle of the night. I know it's last minute … Can we stay with you?" Mommy pleaded.

"Of course, you can come over."

From the backseat window, I looked up at the dark sky, pressed my hands together, and mouthed, *Thank you.*"

We parked at the Bramalea City Centre, caught the next bus, and then took the Go Transit to Celeste's condo in downtown Toronto. For the next eight weeks, until mid-March, we commuted back and forth from Toronto to Brampton and Caledon. We would wake up around four o'clock in the morning to catch the Go Transit to Brampton, where we parked our car overnight. Mom would drive us to our babysitter Rampreet's house in Caledon. My brother and I would walk to our schools, and then we'd stay at an afterschool care program called PLASP at my old school, Peakers Willow, until Mommy picked us up after work. We would grab dinner at Bramalea City Centre and bond as we sat in the parking lot, returning to Aunt Celeste's condo around midnight. And repeat.

One evening, before going to Bramalea City Centre, I asked Mom if we could drive around Ambers Avenue. For reasons unbeknownst to me, I wanted to see the house again.

"Sure," Mom said.

We drove past the house. From the outside, nothing had changed. Everything looked the same, all well put together. But the family that once lived inside was broken.

"I'll tell you one thing … This situation taught me *not* to trust people," Mommy said.

I nodded. I had learned the same thing: to have a very discerning heart. You can't trust everyone. My mom and brother were my *only* family.

As we drove further away from 720 Ambers Avenue, I felt deep abandonment. The feeling of being discarded and unwanted pierced my heart. Grandma didn't care about me. Accepting that reality was hard.

Then, the familiar question: *What's the lesson in this?* That was the last thing I wanted to hear. I was in way too much pain to search for an answer.

You are strong, I told myself. But those words provided me with little comfort. All I wanted to do was weep. The situation Mommy, Jonathan, and I found ourselves in was beyond upsetting. I was hurt. Deeply hurt.

In retrospect, I know why my higher self thought this message was important for me to hear at that moment. It was saying certain life experiences reveal things about yourself. I was reminding myself that I was going to get through this. I was going to gain strength from this.

Auntie Celeste encouraged my brother and me not to bottle things up. She handed us each a black notebook and pen. "Here, if you ever want to write about how you're feeling, this can be your own personal diary."

I didn't understand why she was suggesting I do that. "I'm fine," I told her.

Celeste looked Jonathan and me intently in the eyes, as if she were studying us. "After I discovered the unknown credit cards under my name, I was so angry that I bottled everything up, and it started hurting my stomach. She walked me to her bed and showed me a heating pad she had used to soothe her abdominal pain. "If you need it, you can use it."

"Okay, Auntie," I replied. I thought I was okay. The diary and heating pad were two things I would never use.

Almost every night, Mommy locked herself in Auntie Celeste's bedroom. She was still going back and forth with Grandma and Aunt Felicia via email. Mom had consulted a financial advisor who told her there was no equity in the house and that she should sell it now instead of accumulating interest. Grandma mocked us and refused to sell. She said Mom's name would be removed in 2012 when the mortgage expired. "Good luck finding a place!"

We were enraged.

* * *

We stayed with Aunt Celeste until mid-March, when she moved out of her condo. Mom had found an apartment for us, but we couldn't move in until early April, so we stayed with Mom's best friend, Auntie Grace, in Milton. Mom had met her when she got her job at Wells Fargo shortly before we moved to Caledon, and they stayed in touch ever since.

Auntie Grace, the wife of a husband battling cancer with an eighteen-month-old baby attached to her hip, was the kindest host. She cooked for us, laughed with us, talked with us, and simply let us be. Her support strengthened us. She never mentioned our situation, and we didn't either. We loved living with her.

My last day at school crept up on me fast. The same routine, albeit a bit different since we weren't commuting from Toronto, continued. We woke up early to leave Milton for Caledon, but that would be ending soon. I would be moving to Mississauga, which meant that I'd have to change schools.

If I could have slowed down time, I would have. But, early on in my life, I learned to accept life's transitional phases. *It was what it was.*

Throughout the day, I tried to keep my spirits high. My friends and I did the usual: talk, play, and laugh. But the one person I was looking for never came. Jerod and I were getting close. I'd found out he could draw and had convinced him to draw something for me. In music class, he'd play the piano while my friends and I sang.

"I'm going to move," I told him a few weeks prior.

"No, you're not," Jerod replied, laughing.

I guessed he stayed away on my last day because it was too hard to say goodbye. I understood that. I was pretending with my friends that it was just another day.

Last period was English class. The white clock ticked towards two o'clock. I was running out of time. I'd have to say my farewells to everyone. That was going to be the hardest thing for me to do.

"Guys," Mrs. Padmesh shouted. "As you know, today is Jamilla's last day."

I never liked being the centre of attention, so I tried to act like I didn't hear my name. Mrs. Padmesh gave a lovely speech, and two of my friends stood up and brought a large, colourful card to my desk. It was my classmate's farewell to me.

I tried so hard not to cry as I read their sweet words. My teacher cried. My friends cried. It was difficult.

"I like to move it, move it!" blasted on the school speakers. That was our signal to go home. My last day had ended.

"We're going to walk you to PLASP!" my friends said.

We strolled over to our old school, Peakers Willow, in a huge pack. When we got there, we took turns chatting and embracing. "Bye, everyone," I said, waving. "I gotta go."

Mommy was late picking us up. Life had been so chaotic. Ms. Bonnie, a petite, Italian lady who took care of the kids at PLASP, waited outside with Jonathan and me until Mom pulled up to the entrance.

"Thank you for watching the kids," my mom said.

"Oh, it's no problem, Sandra," she replied. Her eyes brimmed with tears.

We said bye to Ms. Bonnie and watched her drive out of the parking lot hysterically. It was hard to see her wail. We felt bad.

Then we did the same thing: drove off into the sunset.

* * *

And just like that, my life had changed forever. Life, as I knew it, would never be the same. Living in Caledon was the darkest period of my life. These years confused my mind, broke my heart, shattered my faith, and *wounded* my spirit in an indescribable way. These are the chapters of my life that I'll truly never forget. For as much as they strengthened me, they broke me too.

Nine

THE TRICKLE-DOWN
EFFECT

It's not the load that breaks you down, it's the way you carry it....

— Lena Horne

*T*wo worn-out queen-sized beds, Auntie Celeste's blue blow-up mattress, two white lawn chairs, a silver RCA television, a pale brown wooden TV stand, old pots and pans, and clothes. That's what we moved into our desolate apartment with. Nothing else.

Tony, a Jamaican man Mom had befriended at a banquet hall in Caledon, met us at Auntie Grace's house. He was one of the friends who were there, watching everything unfold between us and our relatives. Tony wanted to do anything he could to make the transition to our apartment easy. He and Jonathan jumped into the rental truck filled with our belongings. Mom and I hopped into our Mazda.

"Milla, I think I lost them!" my mom shrieked.

I turned around. "There they are," I pointed. "I think they turned right!"

Mom sped up and drove behind them.

We passed a giant, chestnut landmark inscribed with the words Lysons Landing. I scanned the grotty, dark brown units for building three. We parked beside the curb and got out.

"How was the drive?" Mom asked, greeting the guys at the entrance.

"Every ting good," Tony said.

Mom pulled a key from her purse and opened the door. Jonathan and I rushed into the three-bedroom unit.

"It's huge!" I told Mommy while goofing around in the living room with my brother. "I want the biggest room this time." Mom smiled.

Later that night, I agreed to take the first room. I preferred its petite size. I hung my clothes in my own closet and lined up my shoes. I plastered the walls with large Michael Jackson posters and glow-in-the-dark stars.

"What do you guys want for dinner?" Mom asked. Pizza was our answer. All three of us sat down on the bare oak floor and ate the best Hawaiian pizza we'd ever had.

* * *

On the weekend, Mom took us on the route to school. We strode past the townhouses on Stocksville Avenue, turned left and crossed the next main intersection, near the gas station. "This is the way you'll walk to school," Mommy said, looking at Jonathan and me with a typical mother's concern. "Don't talk to strangers!"

I wanted my first day at Greenwich Public School to be different from the last time. I told myself not to act awkward. I beelined to an empty seat at the back of the room and avoided eye contact with everyone. I kept to myself the entire day.

Afterschool, my brother and I went straight home. Mommy wanted us to stay inside our apartment until she came home from work. That was the rule. "And don't answer the phone unless you recognize my number." So, we sat on our outdoor chairs and played *NBA Street* on my brother's PlayStation, almost every day.

It didn't take us long to make friends. My popular classmate, Tyra, was one of them. I followed her on a short-cut from home to school and found out we lived in the same complex.

"You live here?" she asked me.

I turned my head towards my apartment. "Yeah, I live over there!"

We hit it off after that day. Sometimes, we'd hang out. But most times, I'd chill with my best friend, Nyla. We were in the same class, and she lived a couple buildings down from me.

On the way home from school, Nyla and our other school friends often stopped by the local convenience store. The one that didn't like Black kids roaming around in it. The owners, who were of Asian descent, watched our every move, ensuring we didn't steal their stale candy.

Or we'd hop the rusty fence and walk inside the dark, hollow tunnel in the nearby sewer. "Let's see who gets scared first," someone would say. We'd make it halfway into the sewer. Then someone would make a scary noise, and we'd spin around, screaming. "Ahhh!" Everybody burst out laughing when we got out of there.

My friends kept asking if they could come inside our apartment after school. We had no furniture, nothing on the walls, and barely any food in the fridge or pantry. But I just wanted to feel like a normal child again, so I invited them in.

A blonde-haired classmate of mine named, Adrian, looked around the living room. "Why don't you have any furniture?"

I didn't have a prideful response. "I don't know," I said, and changed the subject.

Adrian and our friends sat on the floor, gossiping about random teenage things. But when I heard stomping upstairs, my attention was abruptly diverted from our conversation.

"They constantly make so much noise," I told my friends, who appeared to be oblivious to the sounds.

My brother chimed in too." Yeah, they're so loud."

"Sorry, it's my little siblings jumping around," Wilma said.

"Oh, it's you guys!" The ruckus had been bothering us ever since we moved in. My spirit filled with rage. "It's okay."

Meanwhile, my mom was still fighting with my grandmother about getting her name removed from the house in Caledon. When she got nowhere with her mother, Mommy decided to file for bankruptcy. I had no idea what she was doing.

"Guys, I'm going to sell the car," Mommy told us.

"No, why?" I whined.

"I can't afford it anymore," she said. "Car insurance is too expensive. We only have two weeks left with the vehicle."

I loved our car. That four-door champagne Mazda3 had carried us through many trials in our lives. I was sure we could figure out a way to keep it.

We couldn't. The truth was, Mommy hadn't decided to sell our vehicle. It was repossessed. When my mom filed for bankruptcy, that meant the majority of her debt would be wiped away, which was a huge relief. No one could hunt her down for overdue payments. But she also had to give up our car. The loan that was taken out when Aunt Felicia and Mom bought the Mazda3 wasn't paid off, so the car belonged to the bank.

Still, on our last day with the car, I pleaded with Mom again.

"I don't want to hear it, Jamilla," she said. "I have to drive it to the Mississauga GO Transit and someone will pick it up from there. I have to go."

I drifted inside our unit, defeated. Now we were going to have to find a way to get around the city without a vehicle. What I didn't understand at the time was that "when you destabilize the mother, you destabilize the children too," as stated by the Honourable Judge Lynn Toler during her appearance on *Divorce Court* (my mom loved to watch it). My relatives did just that.

* * *

Weeks before Auntie Celeste's nuptials with her long-time boyfriend, Eric, my grandfather appeared in my mother's dreams. "He told me to let it go. We have to *forgive* them. We have to *let it go*."

The message from our guardian angel, Papa, was right. I was willing to show my relatives grace because, somehow, from far above, that's what Papa required us to do. I felt that in some weird way he knew we had it in our hearts to do so. But hindsight allows me to see that my grandpa was trying to tell us that forgiveness would set us free.

July 23rd, 2010 came faster than I thought it would. Auntie Celeste would officially marry her beau. It would be a celebration of Congolese and Cypriot cultures. It would also be the first time I would see my relatives after everything that happened that year.

Auntie Celeste, Mommy, and I woke up early that wedding day to get our hair done at a fancy salon. Mya and her older sister Eva, two of Aunt Celeste's Congolese friends she'd met at medical school, picked us up in a black SUV.

At the salon, we were greeted by the owner, who looked every bit like the curvaceous Neo-soul singer Jill Scott. I got a mid-high, curly ponytail done. Mom got a Halle Berry pixie cut, her go-to hairstyle since I was a little girl. Aunt Celeste got a sleek, high bun with a swoop bang. Mya and Eva had their natural hair straightened.

Afterwards, we rushed to 720 Ambers Avenue. Auntie

Celeste hired a make-up artist, who was awaiting our arrival, in my grandmother's master bathroom. Grandma was out getting her hair done, so we had the house to ourselves.

As I walked up the oak staircase for the first time since being cast out overnight, I felt displaced. The house where I once lived was foreign to me now. The energy was uncanny. I didn't like being there.

When I got to the master bathroom, I put a bright look on my face, hoping no one would sense the shift in my energy.

Eric hired someone from his best friend's limousine company, and they drove Aunt Celeste, Mom, Jonathan, and me to the wedding venue. The mood was sombre. We were each thinking our own thoughts.

But we got out of our heads the second we arrived at the destination in downtown Toronto. The main house of the white estate looked like something you'd see in a movie.

"This is so nice," I told Mom.

"It is!" Mommy replied, her eyes filled with the same wonderment as mine.

Mom, Jonathan, and I followed Auntie Celeste into the bridal room. She needed extra time to put on the finishing touch to her wedding day look: her veil. "Let me help you," one of the workers at the estate said. My aunt Celeste sat down on a chair.

"You wanna know something?" She looked closely at my brother and me as the veil was carefully fastened on top of her head.

"What?" we responded.

"You two are the strongest kids I know."

Her words uplifted me. To hear her acknowledge the bravery it took to support her in spite of our pain, discomfort, and apprehension meant a lot to me. For months, I had dreaded the idea of seeing my relatives. Now that we were here, I had no choice. Mommy was the maid of honour. My brother was one of the ring bearers. And I would follow a few moments after them with Uncle Luke's baby boy in my arms. Without a doubt, we needed strength to carry us through.

"Thank you, Auntie," I replied.

You'll be fine. Walk straight, I told myself before making my entrance. I put one foot in front of the other, but I was concerned about my black kitten heels getting stuck in the freshly trimmed grass and dropping my cousin. I hid my fear with a grin. "*Aw!*" everyone said.

The wedding reception was equally breathtaking. The rectangular tables in the ballroom were draped in white silk with a centerpiece of yellow begonias. Mom, Jonathan, and I sat on the opposite side of the room, far away from our relatives and Congolese family friends. No one on either end of the room said a word to each other. It wasn't until someone asked us to come to the table where my grandma, Felicia, and Rick were sitting that we finally came face to face again.

As I approached their table, the pain in my heart and uneasiness in my body momentarily stifled me. *No, I don't want to go closer!*

Then Grandma, dressed in a light pink dress, opened her arms wide and pulled me towards her. A feeling of peace, and deep sorrow, overcame me.

"Hi, Ja-me!" she screamed.

"Hi, Grandma," I replied, holding back tears. I kept our conversation short. I had nothing else to say. Nor did I want to put on an act for everyone to see, even though I felt my grandmother's gesture was sincere. I went back to the kid's table. And despite our trepidation, Mom, Jonathan, and I had a blast dancing the rest of the night.

* * *

Grade seven was the start of a new chapter for me. I no longer had to attend Greenwich Public School, a place I'd grown to dislike. The brown brick aesthetic was bland. My teacher was rude and clearly lacked passion for her job. She went through class lessons without enthusiasm in her eyes or voice. I'd be attending Eastwood Middle School. I couldn't wait!

The night before my first day, I tossed and turned for hours. My internal chatter wouldn't shut off.

My eyes flew open when my alarm clock went off at 6:25 a.m. I'd set it an hour ahead, so I wouldn't be late for school.

"I can't wait to wear my new varsity jacket," I squealed, grabbing it off of the hanger. It was black and white with a purple letter "C" embroidered on the upper right side of the chest. I'd bought it from a small outlet the month before school began.

I was distracted by the concrete block townhouses that reminded me of the one we once had in Aurora and the reddish maple trees around the neighbourhoods I passed during my walk to Eastwood. The radiant views kept my mind occupied, and the light breeze helped cool my nervous system. It was still on overdrive.

My nervousness settled the second I saw my best friend, Nyla, in front of the school.

"Omg, hi, Milla!" she shouted, pressing up against me.

I found the crowd overwhelming. She, on the other hand, was taking in all the familiar faces from Greenwich Public School and all the brand-new faces at Eastwood. I piggybacked off of her infectious energy. Together we skipped to the back of the school, lined up as instructed and filed in with a small group of friends.

While things at school looked bright, living conditions in the apartment continued to plummet. *Drip drip. Drip drip.* Where was it coming from? I didn't see any liquid on the bathroom floor. I tilted my head upwards. *Splash!*

"Yuck," I cried. "There's a leak in the ceiling."

Mom informed ABC Living and repair guys came over. They plastered paint over the ceiling. The intense odor always choked me. But it didn't get rid of the issue. Whatever the unit above was doing trickled down to us.

Then there was the mould issue. The bathroom walls sweated profusely. Inhaling the smell wasn't good for anyone's health. Uncle Eric loaned us his dehumidifier but wanted it back shortly after. For however long we had it, it helped us.

To save more money, my mom decided to disconnect the internet service. I was devastated. But my real breaking point hit the morning when I tried to turn on the television.

"It won't work," I cried.

"Don't be disappointed," Mom said, looking at us with a light in her eyes.

It was hard for me not to be. What was I going to do without a TV to occupy my mind amid the constant banging, stomping, arguing, and music blasting from above? It sounds silly and privileged, but I couldn't cope with life without television. Movies and shows were my escape, my saving grace.

As always, the minute Auntie Celeste caught wind of our television breaking down, she and Uncle Eric came to our rescue. They arrived at our front door after lunch with a silver TV, a light brown wooden dining room table, and two big beaming faces.

We were thankful.

"I'm not feeling well," I told Mom. "I'm not going to school." Each day for about a week, as the leaves slowly unfurled, I locked my bedroom door and lay in bed with the blinds closed. Much like when I was nine years old, I found myself in another bout of depression. No one knew that, not even me.

"Milla, come to school," Nyla demanded.

"No," I responded.

"Where have you been?" Tyra wondered.

In bed. Sleeping. I didn't want to be around people, and I didn't want them to be around me. I wanted to be alone.

I missed my old school. I missed living in Caledon and hanging out with my old friends during recess. I missed my old life.

Even though the overwhelming feeling of melancholy weighed me down, I slowly willed myself to get up. I told myself that as much as I missed my old life, I also missed the things I could experience in the present day. The warmth of the sun's rays hitting my beautiful brown skin. Being around friends who cared about me. I needed to stop being a hermit. Community is what I needed to help me get out of this funk. I wanted to smile again and truly mean it.

But with depression also came anxiety, stress, and a new health problem I had never heard of before, irritable bowel syndrome or IBS. I suffered from unbearable bloating and nonstop constipation. My stomach would be sore for days.

"Mom, I haven't pooped in a while," I confessed when the discomfort became unbearable.

Concern was written all over my mother's face. "That's not good. We'll have to see the doctor."

I realize now, over a decade later, that trauma is what caused this. The very thing that Auntie Celeste told me she had dealt with years ago—stomach issues—began afflicting me. I had shoved all of my anger, sadness, and pain deep within me, and my body was reacting to it.

Add in the constant unsettledness and irritability I felt about the lack of money and food, a random gunshot at dusk, and round-the-clock commotion from the neighbours above us, my body was on fire. No wonder the pain signals in my gut had gone into overdrive. Even with me suppressing my emotions as best as I could, my body kept track.

* * *

We struggled for over a year without a car. Taxis were our number one choice when we needed to travel around town. We'd grab one to go to the grocery store and the coin laundromat, but eventually that became too costly.

"Mommy, I think we might have to start walking," I said. "It'll help us save money." And that's what we did.

When the snow started to fall, Uncle Eric arrived at our apartment driving a beat up, beige Scion. "Hey guys, this is your new car," he said. "It's old, but it drives just as good as new."

That same winter, we sold the Scion. It kept breaking down and we couldn't afford the repairs. Now we were back at square one. No car meant Mommy had to go back to walking to and from the grocery store every two weeks when she got paid.

One Thursday, Mom trudged to Metro before dawn so my brother and I would wake up to the sight of a full fridge. I got up early to get ready for basketball practice. Playing on the school team was a great stress reliever. Looking back, I recognize that playing basketball was not just another outlet for me. Being active also helped me with my IBS and allowed me to release endorphins. As much as I thought I was playing basketball for the love of it, I actually needed it.

As I walked away from my complex, listening to Toni Braxton's newest album, *Pulse*, I saw someone in the distance. I didn't want to draw attention to myself, so I looked down and continued to mind my own business.

But the second I lifted up my head, I knew exactly who the woman was. "Aw, Mommy!" I said, my hand touching my heart.

My beloved mother bravely straightened her spine and held her head high despite the visceral pain on her face from lugging eight heavy bags in six centimeters of unshovelled snow. It's a sight I'll never forget. The strength and resilience of a Black woman is truly immeasurable. My Black queen, my beloved mother, deserves the world. To give my mom just that is my endless vow to her.

Ten

CRASH

*Our greatest glory is not in never falling, but in rising
every time we fall.*

— Confucius

"We're going to move!" I told my friends. Our stay at Lysons Landing was supposed to be short-lived. And in the summer of 2011, it looked like our wish was going to come true.

Grandma came by our apartment with Auntie Celeste. She wanted to have a chat with my mom. It seemed like my grandma wanted to make peace without saying it in those exact words.

I greeted them at the door. They sat down on the leather couch, awaiting Mom's entrance in the living room.

Grandma appeared shaken. Maybe she was taken aback by where we were living. The area. How it looked. The foul smell of mould. The brown stains on the ceiling. The stuffy air.

I don't know what Grandma thought she was going to see. We were living in government-housing again. My mom had been kicked out of her own house in the middle of the night with hardly a penny and two young children. No one cared, except for Celeste and Eric.

Jonathan and I went out, leaving the grown-ups alone to talk. I didn't trust our relatives after what had transpired in Caledon, but I wasn't afraid to leave Mom with Grandma. Auntie Celeste would be there and could protect my mom if another confrontation happened between her sister and their mother.

Grandma said she would help Mom look for a better place, and she was true to her word. We went looking for three-bedroom apartments. I personally wanted to be back in Caledon. Some of our Congolese family friends still lived there. Tantine Pauline was one of them. We ran into her on our way to Fortinos one afternoon.

"I heard you moved to Mississauga with a man," she said.

Mom and I stared at each other confused. When my mom became pregnant with me at nineteen, Grandma had given her an ultimatum. Mom wanted to keep me, so she moved in with my father.

Other than that, she had let her boyfriend, Tez, live with us for a few months when we had our townhouse in Aurora. I was initially confused by Tez's presence in my home and wondered if he was my dad. He'd assure me that he wasn't, that he was just my mother's boyfriend. Once I accepted that he was my mom's new companion, not someone familiar to me, I grew to like him and the cucumber vinegar salad he'd make, especially when I requested it.

But we certainly hadn't moved in with any man, and none was living with us now. Tantine Pauline's comment was odd, but we both knew there were only a few people it could have come from.

Aside from that eyebrow rising exchange, I missed the community vibe. The way people acted. It was friendlier than Mississauga.

Mom didn't. She didn't want to be reminded of the past. Contrary to my mother, I was still holding onto our previous life. I struggled to let go of what once was and accept what we now had.

Even though Mommy didn't want to be back in Caledon, all of us settled on an affordable apartment there. It was much smaller than what we were living in, but that didn't matter to us. It was clean. It was quiet. It was free from mould. It was everything we could have asked for.

"Do you like it?" Mom asked.

"Yes," I replied without hesitation.

Grandma took my mother and Aunt Celeste to the side. "Let's make a rental offer," I heard Grandma mumble. I couldn't make out the rest of their conversation, but things started looking hopeful for us. No one could have told me we weren't going to move.

During the following days, we found out my grandma wasn't able to put the apartment in her name and Celeste declined to take her place. "I can't take on that responsibility right now," she told my mom.

Because my grandma couldn't help us get another apartment, she offered to help us with something else. A reliable vehicle. Without wasting time, we went car shopping. Grandma was a long-standing customer at Northeast Lexus and knew a guy named Ace who could give us a deal.

Ace showed us the cars in the lot. Black. White. Yellow. Red. Four door. Two door. Standard. Manual. What we needed was something simple. After drive-testing a two-door beige Lexus, we were sold. "It drives really well," Mommy said. It was right around our price range, comfortable, and dependable. It was perfect for us. Grandma paid for it in full.

We had that car for three years.

* * *

The day after my sixteenth birthday, Mom headed to work. One second, she was getting ready to make a left turn at a light, and the next second, she was T-boned. While Mom was being pulled out of the Lexus by strangers, Jonathan and I had to have been on her mind. We were at school.

When Mom rushed through the door that evening, we had already been home, awaiting her arrival from work. "Jonathan and Jamilla, come here!" she hollered.

Mom took us to her room, and we sat on the bed. "Why do you have a white band on your wrist?" I asked her.

She took a deep breath. "I got into a car accident on my way to work." Mommy looked intently at my brother and me for a reaction.

My face was blank. My eyes were cold.

"Well … are you okay?" I asked.

"Yes," she said, visibly shaken. "I got us a rental car. Do you want to see it?"

I didn't want to. My mind was in overload every day. I didn't have the mental capacity to process the news Mom dropped onto us. Mommy looked okay. That's all that mattered to me.

We went outside and sat in the car. I could tell my mom was trying to gauge how much to tell us about the accident. She watched for our reactions.

"I know it's a lot … How are both of you feeling?" she asked.

"I'm tired but okay," I said.

My brother struggled to speak. "Yeah."

As we walked to our unit, I mouthed, "I'm happy you're okay, though, Mom." Momentary joy lifted her cheeks.

This is, yet again, another thing we'll have to fight for, I told myself. *But we'll get through this. We'll get the car accident settlement money soon.*

How I saw it then was that life is all about choices. At this moment, I had two. I could either maintain a positive or negative attitude.

I see now that my perspective was my way of coping with life's challenges. Finding the positive in experiences helped me stay afloat when I felt like the pressure from my circumstances was going to drown me. It was a helpful strategy, one that I don't regret and will always use. However, in my efforts to stay mentally resilient and avoid wallowing in self-pity, I neglected to acknowledge and address my emotional needs.

I hopped on the yellow school bus the next day pretending like nothing happened until I saw my classmates during biology. "Guys, my mom got into a car wreck," I told them. "Why are you smiling?" they asked me.

It was a defence mechanism. My way of trying to minimize the upsetting situation. If I could convince myself that what my mom went through wasn't so bad, then I could move forward with life. This way was much easier for me. For everyone. Until it wasn't.

* * *

Each day, thoughts of the car accident replayed in my mother's mind. She was too scared to drive. More concerningly, her health deteriorated. Her back and legs hurt. All she could do was lie on the couch. She slept in the living room because her bedroom was filled with mould.

"How are you feeling?" I asked Mom every morning.

"Oh, I'm feeling okay," she replied.

I could tell by the look on my mom's face, the faintness in her voice, and the stillness in her body that she was in agony. Mommy had ringing in her ears, discomfort in her legs, swelling in her feet, and a misaligned vertebrae in her spine. Eventually, she was diagnosed with a chronic disorder called fibromyalgia.

Mom had to go on short-term disability soon after. While she recuperated at home, her paycheques dwindled. Mommy still got paid every two weeks, but we continued to run out of food about four days before the next paycheque, which varied. Her job would underpay her on occasion, leaving us awaiting the monies owed on the next paycheque.

We lived on plain rice with sugar and margarine, or pasta with canned tomato sauce if we had any. When we didn't, I'd open our outdated refrigerator and all I could see was my own reflection. Those days were hard. I'd go to bed early to make the days go faster, but sometimes the time dragged. *Hold on*, I'd tell myself. *You can do it.* Again, mental strength was key.

Whenever Auntie Grace or Tony could, they'd help Mommy buy groceries. When Auntie Grace found out we didn't have any food in our refrigerator or cabinets, she pulled up to our apartment with large bags of food. There are no words to describe how grateful we were.

As usual, she was modest. "You're welcome, Sandra. Don't be afraid to tell me when you need help. You and the kids eat up. I have to go make a meal for my boys now. We'll talk soon!"

My friends at school helped too, although they didn't know it. More than once I was served a replica of our schools' infamous stuffed Jamaican patties with lettuce, tomato, cheese, and mayo at a friend's house.

Out of everyone, Tony was the person we relied the most on. He was a single father, raising two young boys, and understood the struggle of trying to provide for them. Tony would come over to teach me how to cook a dish with rice and peas and savory chicken, or talk with us, especially me, about being cautious of boys who might have ill intentions. He wanted to give me advice on guys since I wasn't getting it from a father at home.

"Leave the boys alone. Focus on school. No one can take away what's in here," he'd tell me, pointing at his head.

* * *

"Mom, we have no toilet paper!" I cried as I sat on the toilet.

"I know. We'll have to wait until Thursday," my mom responded.

None of us had money. Heck, I didn't even own a debit card yet. But I didn't see how waiting was possible, so I came up with an idea. "Mom, I'll take some toilet paper from school."

She neither agreed nor disagreed. The next day, I set my pride aside, went into a grey bathroom stall and put a roll of toilet paper into my backpack.

Simultaneously, my mom was going through bouts of "brain fog." Before the accident, she'd been working toward a real-estate license. Auntie Grace was making good money, and Mom planned to use the second income to get us out of Lysons Landing within the next two years. It seemed like a fantastic plan. My mom had the personality and charisma when she wasn't overly timid. But now that Mom was having trouble remembering information, she had to put her plans on hold.

That left me wondering, more than ever, what more I could do. Waiting every Thursday to buy food wasn't going to work for me anymore, and neither was taking toilet paper from school. Something had to give.

Eleven

OLDEST SIBLING WOES

Elder daughter syndrome: you're not allowed to need, you're not allowed to want. All you have to do is give, all you have to do is serve in your position because you can see that there is a lack.

— Courtney Daniella Boateng

I entered the living room and saw Mommy lying on the couch. I looked at her and announced, "I'm going to get a job."

"No, Milla, just be a kid. Don't worry about that," she said.

I wasn't going to listen to her. You see, the problem wasn't about my mom's occupation or how much she made. She worked at a healthcare company and made middle-class income, but bills took all of it away. We lived paycheque to paycheque. Mom just needed some help.

Suddenly, thoughts of my father entered my mind. It was the first time it happened without being prompted by my mother, relatives, or strangers in a long time. *What would my life have been like if Dad had stepped up years ago?*

To an outsider, I probably appeared composed at that moment, but inside, I felt every cell in my body firing up, and knew I wasn't going to calm down anytime soon.

Maybe Mom should've gotten Dad to pay child support, I told myself. *If she had, life wouldn't have been so hard all these years.*

I shook my head. *No, no, no. Everything happens for a reason.* In my heart, I had to believe that. Who knew what would have happened if Mom had sought child support from Dad.

Here I was thinking that things would have been better, but there was another possibility: things might have been worse. What if Dad wasn't financially stable? What if he didn't want to help Mommy and fought her in court about paying back child support? Grappling with both scenarios made me certain that God had divinely planned out this part of my story. This was the way things were meant to be. There was no reason to question that.

My outrage sizzled. And within an instant, I forgave my father for his financial absence in my life.

In the weeks to come, I made a résumé. I didn't have much job experience; I was a newspaper carrier when I was fourteen years old. But I hoped someone would give me a chance.

I had no luck. Places either gave me no response or they wanted years of experience. How was I supposed to get experience if no one would hire me? Job hunting sucked.

More discouraging than that was seeing some of my peers getting jobs with ease when they didn't need them. They just wanted their own spending money. But I *needed* a job.

My media arts teacher, Mr. Good, offered to assist me with my resume. "Every curriculum vitae I've made for someone landed them a job. I'll fix it up for you," he told me.

I went to Canadian Tire for the second time with my new CV in my hand. A few weeks later, in May, I got a call. "Hey, Jamilla, this is Tessa. I'd like to offer you the cashier position if you still want it." I took the job without blinking twice.

On the weeks Mom didn't get paid, I stepped in and gave her $100 for groceries, or more if she needed to pay for something else. I also tried my best to save for university and put money aside for a rainy day so Mom and I wouldn't worry.

Having money saved up put me at ease. I would try to save $1,000 in my bank account, but when it came time to help with the rent, I had to start back at zero. It stressed me out.

As my mother so often reminded me, "Money comes and goes." After what transpired in Caledon, Mommy understood a teaching about money that I hadn't fully grasped yet. Money is needed to pay for necessities and to take care of responsibilities, but we shouldn't attach ourselves to it. So, whenever I felt dejected and frustrated, that saying rang in my ears. Yes, the money was gone. But surely it would come again.

In two months, I told myself. *I should be able to make $1,000 back.*

Most times, I wasn't able to. No matter how many times I declined to accompany my friends after school to Dairy Queen for a caramel shake, talked myself out of buying food when I was hungry during my lunch break at work, or put off buying underwear and socks, the money came and went, sometimes faster than I could count.

But knowing that we were okay, that I could lessen my mom's financial load, that my brother didn't have to grow up fast like I did, brought me comfort.

Pressure, which stemmed from lack, was the only thing that made me feel the opposite: heartache. I now recognize that, because I was the oldest sibling, I took on the role of the "fixer," and it overwhelmed me. As the eldest daughter, all you can do is sit in your role and oversee everyone and everything, so that if someone (and it *can't* be you) drops the ball or something unforeseen happens, you're there to pick up the missing pieces.

In doing so, we sometimes become passive, a behaviour I picked up from my mother. I assumed that no one would help me, either because they couldn't, or they didn't think it was necessary. As a consequence, I learned not to ask people for help, even when I desperately needed it. I became unassertive, financially independent, and disheartened.

I was giving Mom $100 for groceries every two weeks, like clockwork, but the number of grocery bags didn't add up. Something was off.

"The cost of living has gone up," Mommy would tell me. It had. Yet the feeling of being taken advantage of and unappreciated crept over me.

Mommy picked me up from work one night. "Milla, look," she said, showing me a small, white purse. I had complained to a friend weeks before then about my growing suspicions. "You should say something," they advised me. Once I saw the Guess purse, it was time.

"Mom, that money could have been used for groceries," I told her, my voice shaky.

"I can treat myself! The girls at work make their children contribute financially too. I don't see a problem with giving me $100 every two weeks," she shouted.

At my expense! That wasn't fair.

"I could've saved that money, Mom!" It was the first time I gathered the courage to challenge my mother. Even though the conversation went nowhere. It resulted in us retreating to separate corners of our apartment and not speaking to each other for days. I was proud of myself for speaking up and not shoving my feelings away.

Without question, I wanted my mom and Jonathan to have everything they ever wanted. However, looking back, I realize that whether it was Mom getting a new purse or Jonathan wanting to play on a soccer team (which hindsight allows me to see was his own outlet, providing a sense of community with a father-figure coach and supportive teammates), the person most affected was me. I was the one picking up the slack. And I didn't want to be the one focused on lack: the fear of drowning in debt, not having good food to eat, or struggling to keep a roof over our heads.

I put my wants on the back burner to help us. Even now, I wouldn't change that. I loved helping out. But sometimes, I wished that I had the space to put myself first without feeling any stress, regret, or guilt. I just wanted to be a worry-free kid.

Twelve

MIRRORS?

Children are great imitators, so give them something great to imitate.

— Unknown

$\mathcal{S}$ibling conflict is a tale as old as time. I was twelve years old when the rift between my brother and me began.

One afternoon, we arrived home from Greenwich Public School. I placed my backpack on the ground. Jonathan stepped towards me and said, "Listen, Jamilla!"

He wanted to discuss an issue with me. I can't remember what it was, but the firmness in my brother's voice meant he was serious.

I stared at him perplexed. *What's going on? Why is he acting this way?*

Before we moved to Mississauga, the two of us had rarely fought. With only eighteen months between us, we were as close as twins. We were each other's best friends.

I was used to my brother's personality. He was a free-spirited child, something I admired and secretly wished I could be more like. Although I found it frustrating to handle Jonathan's defiant ways at times, I grew to accept his nature.

When I became a teenager, my attitude changed towards him. I began to see my brother as the typical annoying younger sibling. I'd get embarrassed by Jonathan mouthing off to people and later showing off his butt crack, even if it made our friends laugh. I had been looking forward to attending Eastwood Middle School without him in the fall.

Attending a new school meant I could focus on myself and take a break from being the responsible big sister. I could finally be a carefree kid. I couldn't wait to experience real freedom.

There was a great price I paid for having that mindset.

From the day of my initial tiff with my brother and onwards, I'd be chased from our living room to the dining room, which were a short distance from each other, back and forth. I would hide behind the small space in between the wall and our couch.

To "defend" myself if things were to ever go too far, sometimes I'd grab the remote and whack him with it. The way I saw it then was that my actions were justified. And yet I've come to realize that, despite my heart hammering away in my chest and panic rushing through my veins, grabbing the remote and whacking my brother with it was inexcusable.

"Leave me alone, Jonathan!"

He would corner me. "You need to listen to me! You're not listening to me!"

I didn't want to. From my point of view, all of that commotion to get my listening ear was unnecessary. The only thing loud talking did was unnerve my spirit, and in all honesty, I didn't know why. My strong reactions to confrontations had always puzzled me, but no matter how deep I dug to find the answer, I couldn't figure out the reason behind it. I just wanted the shaky feeling in my body to stop, and for my brother to leave me alone.

Regardless of my efforts, funnily enough, that word *listen* still rings in my twenty-six-year-old ears. I now understand that my brother was simply asking to be heard, almost screaming to be heard. But I didn't have the mental or emotional capacity to give him what he needed—emotional support.

I became cold and distant. I intentionally tried to block out the noises above my head and the ones that came from my brother's emotional outbursts, all of which made me irritable, so that I could free up mental space for myself. Acting this way helped me stay sane. It gave me some level of control over my life.

Besides, what did emotional support look like? If I couldn't provide myself with that, there was no way I could give it to my brother. I had no clue what it was or how to give it to someone. I was trying to survive the best way I knew how.

After what happened in Caledon, none of us had a chance to heal from it. Life continued on. This was our new reality, and we had to adjust to it fast. But the damage it created was huge.

All my life, my brother was used to receiving attention from the adults in our family. When we moved to Lysons Landing, that stopped. There was no more extended family.

It was just the three of us now. But with Mom working for eight hours a day and me unable to support my brother in the way I had done before, he started to struggle. Jonathan had lost his extra cushioning, and he was displeased about it.

Most importantly, he missed the way our relationship was: the closeness between us, the times we'd play with each other and laugh until our stomachs hurt. He longed for the best friend, playmate, and confidant I used to be, not the emotionally unavailable big sister who had to take on the roles of provider, advisor, and second parent quickly. Without all of that normalcy in his life, Jonathan had a huge void, and an even bigger desire to be heard and seen again.

I couldn't see that. I thought my brother was acting crazy. And I'd shout that word at him during multiple feuds.

"No, I'm not," he'd reply, his voice rising by the syllable. "Don't say that!"

Crazy is a term I'd later regret using. My brother wasn't crazy. He was simply hurting.

What I know now that I wish I knew then is that we were taking our anger, pain, and resentment out on each other. Who else could we release those emotions onto? It was all too much for us to cope with.

I continued to flounder. A part of me felt fragile during the arguments with my brother. I didn't like that feeling, so I felt that I had to alter my nature. Appearing calm wasn't working in my favour. I had to become the fight instead of the flight.

Little by little, I stopped backing down when verbal disagreements occurred between us. We'd take turns firing words. Sometimes, it was about more serious things, and other times, it was childish sibling mocking.

"You're not smart," I'd say.

"I'm smarter than you," he'd reply.

Why did I say those words? *Jealousy* and *insecurity*. I knew my baby brother was smarter than me in ways I could never be. Yes, I had the "book smarts." But him? He had it overall. I knew it. And he knew it, too.

In time, Mom slowly began to pick up on cues. I had been trying my best to mask the truth about the problems my brother and I were facing, but shortly after our first spat, Mom randomly told us details about our father's relationship with his sister Ursula.

"They'd fight violently," Mom said. "Don't ever put your hands on each other."

Looking back on it, hearing this revelation at that exact moment couldn't have been a coincidence. My brother and I needed to be told that our paternal family also had a history of discord. Knowing this information would hopefully lead us to breaking a generational cycle on both sides of our family.

After that day, Mom could tell if something had happened when she arrived home from work. The atmosphere would feel heavy when she strolled into the apartment. I'd usually be sitting on a dining room chair, trying to complete homework or another task. Or one of us would be in our bedrooms.

When I was in my room, I'd overhear the conversations between my mother and brother in the living room. As they talked, I'd lay on my bed and let the old school R&B music drown out the angry voice in my head.

"What happened, Jonathan?" Mom would ask.

"Jamilla … she said *this* … she did *that*," he'd reply with conviction in his voice. "She's prideful. She never apologizes."

"I'll talk to her," Mom would say.

From there, Mommy would get my side of the story. I never felt completely heard. For the most part, I thought my mom was excusing my brother's behaviour.

"Well, you shouldn't have said anything under your breath." she'd say. "You're antagonizing him."

There were times when I admit that I did egg my brother on. I could have ended our conflicts earlier by not having to get the last word. In those instances, I wasn't innocent. I have to own that.

Still, I struggled to defuse the arguments.

"When he gets like that, don't say a word," Mom would tell me.

"Don't fight," Tony would say. "It's not worth it. Be a good girl and go to your room."

Taking either person's advice didn't change a thing. Whether I walked away from a dispute and headed towards my bedroom without saying a word, tried to stick up for myself and responded to Jonathan directly, or mumbled words underneath my breath, it was still an issue.

Everything was "your mouth" or "you did this or that." But when is the other party looked at? When do we look at the man and ask: *Why are you behaving this way? Why do you think it's acceptable to behave poorly when you're angry?*

Back then, I strongly believed that my Black mother, like many others, unknowingly instilled destructive habits in their sons. I understood the reasoning: it's difficult for Black boys and men to navigate a world that unfairly perceives them as scary, violent, and rude. So, they need to be uplifted and loved. However, as I saw it, coddling and overlooking their mistakes, instead of holding them accountable, was detrimental.

The onus should've been equally placed on each party. That way, Jonathan and I would've learned how to self-reflect and take accountability. Mom wanted us to do that when she'd suggest we reflect on what happened. In those moments, it just seemed like the focus was only on me no matter what I did or didn't do.

* * *

I, in no way, was completely guiltless in all of this, as you see. The things that I said and did to my brother were unkind. Now I'm aware of how powerful and strong words can be. Words have the ability to build people up or break them down.

The power of my tongue is something I don't take lightly anymore. So, I take responsibility for how my words have wounded my brother as we grew up. No matter how he was acting, that doesn't justify my cold behaviour towards him.

On reflection, I recognize that certain behaviours I displayed damaged my relationship with my brother, and even my mother. I could have made more effort to be the one to break the ice by apologizing first, rather than feeling justified in not wanting to engage with them after disagreements. That was emotional violence, and it was wrong of me to treat them that way.

I will always be a work in progress, so I'm still learning how to not be passive aggressive. Regardless of whether or not I have a conversation about what transpired with the person I disagree with, I don't want to participate in toxicity anymore.

Aside from my own introspection, my biggest takeaway is how important learning to understand one another is. It can lead to peace between people. I know there was no way I could have come to that conclusion during my youth. I didn't have the necessary tools or feel the need to fully see my brother's perspective. But now I do.

All those years, my brother and I didn't mean each other any harm. What we went through in our relationship was a culmination of built-up repression of emotions. And a lack of real, honest communication.

Were we nurtured to be this way? We had no good examples of what it looked like to express ourselves healthily during conflicts. Now, I undeniably know that what we witnessed as children impacted us. We internalized certain behaviours from our relatives without realizing it. Add all of that together with the environment we lived in, it was a recipe for disaster.

Now that we recognize these patterns, my brother and I are trying to break those generational cycles of toxicity that Mommy believes our great-grandfather and Papa prayed about before they passed away. For the next generation to carry on the task of being light workers, to finish the mission they were not fully able to complete in their lifetimes.

What I do know for certain is that the love my brother and I have for each other runs deep. We didn't always have the healthiest methods of communicating our emotions and opinions, and we're still working on it. However, through empathizing with each other's different perspectives, forgiveness and grace have been found. And we've finally been able to show each other what we were searching for all those years as we grew up—true understanding.

My brother and I during the years we grew up in Aurora. He was my best friend.

Thirteen

THE WAITING GAME

There are certain life lessons that you can only learn in the struggle.

— Idowu Koyenikan

Pruning is the process of ridding trees of all dead, diseased, and damaged branches. The gardener's goal is to minimize the number of stems competing with the centerpiece, giving the tree its strength.

* * *

Shortly after Mom gained her confidence on the road, she got into another car accident. Mom was driving a champagne Mazda3 (yes, we bought the same model and colour vehicle) on the highway when a wheel on a truck flew off and hit the car. It was a write-off.

This time around, it didn't take long for Mommy to receive compensation. The money she got wasn't enough, but it helped us buy a used car.

We drove to Barrie with Mom's Guadeloupean boyfriend of three years. His name was Louis. The four of us wanted to check out a silver Honda Accord Hybrid an elderly gentleman owned.

"It's in good condition," the man told us. "Drive it if you want."

We hopped in the car and drove it around the block a few times. "It's good," Louis said. "You should get it, Madame Kabongo."

Things in life were pretty good after that. Louis would stop by Lysons Landing once or twice a week and park his white Audi next to our building. He and Mom would sit in his car and chat for an hour, or they'd go out on dates.

On one of those outings, he asked my mom a question about me.

"Louis asked if you knew how to love a man," Mom said.

His question took me by surprise. For one, Louis and I hadn't formed a bond due to a lack of effort on both of our parts. I didn't want to get close to him out of fear he'd want to step in and play daddy. I had already gone through so much life without one. Besides, I already had a father figure, someone I connected with years ago: my mom's soft-spoken Jamaican friend, Tony.

There were also situations that made me dislike Louis. For my mom's thirty-eighth birthday celebration, I surprised her by inviting him to Moxies. When the waiter asked if I wanted a to-go box for my food, Louis told me it was unladylike to take one. Then one winter weekend, he had asked my single mother to borrow our car for a trip to Montréal when he could have driven his own. I perceived both behaviours as uptight and selfish.

But perhaps Louis didn't want to be around me due to his own childhood fear of abandonment and rejection. He had lost his mother at a young age and had to take care of himself when his dad remarried. More concerning, maybe, he had assumed that because of my mother's past with my father, I had built my walls so high that no man could break through them.

"I think so, Mom. I grew up around men," I replied.

I still ruminate about Louis' question.

* * *

During the holidays and birthdays, we'd attend family gatherings at one of our relatives' houses. We'd come even when we didn't want to or didn't have the money to spend on gas. I'd go for one reason: my cousins.

"I haven't seen them in a while," I'd say.

Mom would nod. "I'm going for the young ones, too."

On Christmas day in 2014, we gathered at the house in Caledon. We didn't want to come empty handed, but we had no money for gifts and scrambled to find change to purchase a turkey. Mom made a mean one.

Aunt Celeste was now a mother to a one-year-old daughter. No one could deny how much she had helped us over the years. She had let us live with her when we were kicked out of our house, bought Jonathan and me journals, paid for our groceries and swimming lessons, helped Mom buy a couch when we moved, and brought over a dining room table and a TV when ours broke down. But we had hoped that our love and the turkey we'd bring would mean more than not bringing a gift.

We were greeted at the front door by Grandma. She waved her hands. "Come in."

Tense and agitated energy always had a way of permeating every corner of the house and seeping through my pores. But that evening, things appeared light.

In retrospect, I think that's what I wanted to believe. The reality is, it didn't matter if the turkey Mom made had been gobbled up and no one said a word about us not bringing gifts. When we said our goodbyes and returned home, I felt like I always had after family gatherings: depleted.

Mom told our relatives when we had made it home safely. My grandma was the first to respond. Aunt Felicia and Uncle Rick were next. But there was no response from Aunt Celeste.

"I won't think too much into it," Mom said. "I'm going to wash the dishes."

My brother left our apartment to visit a friend's house. I stayed home, pacing back and forth in the living room.

When Mom's phone rang, I walked into the kitchen. "Aunt Celeste texted you."

Mom turned off the tap and read aloud the message:

When Jamilla was a baby,
I took care of her when you, Marcus, and Ursula
got into a fight.
Remember who helped you!
Eric expects you to buy gifts for his daughter.

My mouth dropped. In my heart, I'd known that Aunt Celeste wasn't going to let my mom get off easy for not bringing her daughter a gift. I didn't understand why. She'd known how much we had struggled financially. Where did she think we were going to get the money from?

This puzzle piece was one that my mom least wanted me to find out. If Mom had it her way, she would've kept that secret close to her chest for the rest of her life. She couldn't now.

Mommy felt the need to explain the text, so we went to her room and sat on the bed. I had tears in my eyes as Mom told me how Ursula, my father's sister, had picked up a knife, pointed it at him, and then verbally attacked my mom when she tried to diffuse the fight. A part of me wanted to know everything. And yet, I reacted the same way I did when Mommy first told me about her abusive relationship with my dad a few days before my sixteenth birthday.

My breathing got heavy. "I don't think I can handle this … Don't tell me more."

I left Mom's room, prepared myself for bed, and wept for hours.

* * *

The house in Caledon was sold in 2015. Grandma didn't tell us. Auntie Celeste sent my mother an email. No apology for her previous words was included in it. Now that this chapter of our lives had fully closed, Mom, Jonathan, and I could do something we had already done: move on from 720 Ambers Avenue.

Grandma moved up north to Sudbury and then La Prairie, a city in southwestern Québec. After her first visit to Lysons Landing, she had been phoning us. I'd ask if I could stay with her during summer or winter breaks. Our relationship was never the same. But whenever I would get one-on-one time with her, there was a chance I'd have the nurturer back. Only then would I feel safe enough to be the grandchild. So when she'd offer to pay for the train ticket, I wouldn't think twice about taking the four-hour ride to her house.

At Grandma's, I would sleep until noon and wake up to a plate of fruits, breakfast sausages, my grandma's famous eggs, and her favourite whole grain bread.

"Do you want margarine?" she'd ask me.

I'd usually decline her offer and spread my toast with orange marmalade. I've loved that jelly since I was a child.

Before sunset, we'd take a walk and inhale the fresh Québec air. "Let's go see Tantine Jolène," my grandma would say. "I haven't seen her in a while." I was always happy to join her.

When I returned home from Grandma's house one summer, there was news for me. Wilma and her family, the turbulent neighbours who lived above us, had moved. My eyebrows furrowed. I couldn't understand how they got out of this miserable place faster than we did.

We must've done something really bad in our past lives, I thought. I shook my head. Living at Lysons Landing wasn't a punishment. Still, I couldn't understand what the purpose in all of this was.

Was it about gaining strength, faith, humility, and building character? There was something about the longevity of this experience that didn't make sense to me. Nine years? By now, I was sure we understood the teachings. When was Mom going to get the car accident settlement money so we could move?

Perhaps I couldn't get all the answers I was seeking yet. But one thing I knew for certain was that I had to get my head out of this dump. I couldn't let myself fall victim to our financial circumstances or stay stuck on Wilma's family moving before us. I had to keep pushing forward.

* * *

On New Year's Eve of 2018, we huddled and held each other's hands. "This is *our* year! We're going to move!"

We were manifesting change. No one could tell me otherwise, not even the Creator. I was determined to make a positive change in our lives. Somehow, some way it was going to happen.

At home, it was just Mom and me. My brother moved to Guelph to study urban planning. Oddly, the distance was creating a closer bond between us. We'd call each other on FaceTime to catch up on life every week.

"Hey, big head," I'd say.

"Your upper lip smells," he'd reply, laughing.

Little did I know, Jonathan was struggling financially in Guelph, and so were we at home. I was working two minimum wage jobs and attending five university classes.

In the midst of all of that, there was an issue with the Honda Accord. The pro with having a hybrid vehicle was that it was good on gas. Putting $40 in the tank lasted

Mom two weeks. The con was that it would take a while for the car to warm up when it was brisk.

One morning, Mom put the car key into the ignition switch. It wouldn't turn on.

Mom rushed inside the apartment. "Milla, the car isn't starting!"

"Let me try."

I had no luck starting it either. I had claimed 2019 as ours, and I meant that. For this to be happening at the start of the year, made my heart sink.

"We can't keep doing this!" I told Mom, my voice riddled with despondency. "We'll have to find a way to get a brand-new car."

My goal was to put the vehicle in my name only. If we were going to move, that meant Mommy couldn't have anything attached to her name. She already had two strikes: being Black and having previously filed for bankruptcy. Over the past few years, the bankruptcy had prevented Mom from obtaining credit cards and rebuilding her credit history with banks.

For three days, my mom and I woke up at dawn. We would put ourselves together and order Ubers to take us to car dealerships. Our first trip was to Honda. We drove a black Honda Civic on the main road.

"It drives really nice," Mom said.

We sat down on chairs in the sales department. The saleswoman asked, "Will the loan be in both of your names?"

"No, it'll be in my name," I said.

When they ran my credit, everything was fine. I had gotten a credit card when I was seventeen and built a solid history. But the manager had one request for me before the ink was almost dry. "Is there any way you can find a co-signer?"

That was the last thing I wanted to be asked. "No, I don't know anyone else. It has to be me only."

The next day, my thoughts were crowded. Besides Tony and Auntie Celeste, who had tightly embraced me at a family event I was hesitant to attend after what had occurred between her and my mom in 2014 (I saw that gesture as her way of apologizing to me for her indelicate words towards my mother), I couldn't think of anyone.

Then Grandma popped up in my head. Outside of Aunt Celeste, I didn't want to involve any of my relatives in helping us get an automobile again. I didn't want them involved in our business, but my back was against the wall.

I called Grandma. "Can you co-sign on a car with me? I've wanted one for a while."

"Um … can I think about it?" she asked.

"Of course," I answered. That meant her answer was no, meaning Mommy and I were back at square one. *What will we do?*

I looked up at the moving clouds and said a prayer. It had been a very long time since I had last asked the Creator for help.

Mom sat on the couch. "Don't forget the Uber driver gave us his cousin's number at Toyota." The first day we went car shopping, we met an outgoing Indian Uber driver. We had felt that it was a divine interaction.

At the Toyota dealership, a man dressed in a black suit approached us. I introduced Mom and myself.

"My cousin told me about you. Don't worry. I'll take care of you," Sharanpreet said.

That's exactly what he did. I leased my first vehicle, a blue Toyota Corolla in my name only. It was approved in three days.

As I waited for Sharanpreet's call about when I could pick up the car, I went through a series of emotions. Anger was the most intense one. My blood was boiling because I had finally allowed myself to sit in the reality of something I had overlooked for a long time.

I'm in this situation because of my relatives, I told myself. *If they hadn't set us back by years, my life wouldn't have been this hard! I wouldn't have had to fight for everything!*

Don't get me wrong, I was appreciative that the Creator came through for me and knew that's what I should focus on. But I felt that selfishness from people in my life had led me to years of heartache. Now that everything had worked out in my favour, I was contemplating on whether it was time to cut my relatives off for good.

One afternoon, before making my final decision, I called my uncle Rick. I stayed in contact with him because of my love for my cousin Angel.

"I've been there before," he told me. "I wanted to cut them off too."

"For real?"

"Yes, I did," he said. "If you can live without talking to them for the rest of your life, then do that. But only if you won't regret it."

I chose not to cut ties with them. Instead, I distanced myself from everyone except for Uncle Rick and Aunt Celeste. I wanted to focus on my real family, Mommy and Jonathan, and remove all outside noise so I could concentrate on moving.

* * *

For my twenty-first birthday, I got an unexpected gift. I thought my mom was going to pick me up from work, but when I got into the car, a tall man was driving it.

"Surprise!" my brother shouted.

I paused. "You told me you couldn't make it for my birthday!"

Jonathan giggled. "I lied. God bless you for getting the car, Milla."

My brother's one week stay became permanent. He didn't want to attend school in Guelph anymore.

I looked at my brother, taken aback. He seemed to be excelling in school and enjoyed most of his classes. "Why?" I asked him.

"There's one course that's too difficult. The teacher is giving me and my friend Kaden a hard time. We can't pass the course."

I understood. Not all professors made learning easy. Even though Jonathan didn't want to continue his studies, I was content to have all three of us under one roof again.

Reading week approached two weeks after my brother's unforeseen announcement. I looked forward to having a break from school, my living situation, and the stress of finding a new vehicle. I made plans without hesitation.

I went to Aunt Celeste's house. Her daughter and my uncle Rick's two daughters, Angel and her half-sister, whom I asked Celeste to invite over, kept me company. For dinner, I made salt and pepper chicken wings and fries. At night, we played dress-up and watched *Kim Possible*.

After my cousins went to bed, Aunt Celeste and I sat at the dining room table. I looked at her, knowing she had once been my safe space, and that I could open up fully to her without fear of my words being shared.

"Life has been so hard since we moved to Lysons Landing," I said, holding back tears. "There were times when we barely had food."

Tears filled up her eyes. "Why didn't you tell me this? I would've helped."

"You already did a lot for us. We didn't want to be a bother.

I took a deep breath and continued. "You know … One thing that the car situation revealed to me is that the family set us so far backwards."

"Well … not all hands were clean."

Her words felt like a slap to my face. Was she justifying what happened to us?

My intention was to express my pain of feeling stuck in my circumstances, not to critique my mother. I knew my mom had her faults. When we lived in Aurora, she had lost her temper and spanked me after she believed I'd misbehaved. During the end of our days in Caledon, she had been speaking loudly at times. In Mississauga, she bought a purse when money could've been saved. Worst of all, she didn't make the best choices with men. No one seemed to get over her relationship with my father. But at that moment, I also understood why Mommy told me she had felt judged by Celeste for years and regretted my conversation with her.

Even when the right was staring Auntie Celeste in the face, in secret, she had always taken the side of the wrong because of the feelings she had carried towards my mother, whom she felt was unfairly put on a pedestal by others since they were children. And because Celeste felt that she had to replace her older sister's role when my mom was forced by their mother to leave the family nest at nineteen when she got pregnant with me. Aunt Celeste wanted to be what my mom should've been in the eyes of their mother: the perfect daughter.

"I went to medical school for our mom! I got married for her! And still that wasn't enough!" Celeste said, fighting to hide her visceral pain. "Your Mom isn't perfect! She stopped paying the bills."

In my eyes, Mom had every right to do so. I wasn't going to look at her sideways for doing that. My mother did what anyone who had been financially violated would have done: look out for themselves and their two children.

"We're going to move this year," I told her. "I'm sure of that."

Aunt Celeste shook her head. "No, you won't."

"Yes, we will," I said.

* * *

Out of the blue, as the bright stars beamed through the night sky, my brother ran into someone unexpected from the past. It was Wilma. She saw Jonathan and ran towards him.

"I left my mother's place," she said.

"Really?" my brother replied.

She cried, "Yes, I've turned to the streets to make money. How did y'all do it?"

Her question was something I would've never imagined her asking any one of us. The person who belonged to the family that contributed to making my living environment hell for eight years was looking my brother in the face and asking him for advice even though we hadn't made it out yet. A part of me wanted to scream, *The audacity!* While another part of me thought, *Life is so interesting.*

"Want more for your life," he told her. "Don't settle for less."

You see, my wise, beautiful brother was able to bestow grace and counsel to our former neighbour because he had found beauty in the struggle, much faster than I did. He understood that the perceived obstacles and blockages during certain stages in our lives weren't enemies like I once viewed them. They were building blocks.

Those experiences, coming from a large house and transitioning back to living in government housing, gave us different perspectives. Because we had known the meaning of having more when we were younger, we were able to see and want more for ourselves as we grew older. For that reason, that nightfall, my brother was able to offer Wilma a teaching that I hope she will take on her journey for a lifetime.

Fourteen

A PROMISE FULFILLED

There's a light at the end of every tunnel.

— Universal Quote

*I*t was in March of 2019 when Mom got a call from her lawyer Lana. "The big guy wants to settle, Sandra." My mom had been tired of the back and forth for the last five years and agreed to finalize the settlement.

On the day Mom was to pick up the cheque, she woke up early and prayed. She didn't want to go to the lawyer's office alone, so I skipped school.

We took a taxi to downtown Toronto. Mom was feeling emotional and preferred to be driven by someone who was less jittery than us. There was barely any traffic on the route to the office. We arrived there at 10 a.m. sharp.

The receptionist greeted us and pointed to Lana's room. Mom went in. I sat on a bench, admiring the shiny black and gold marble walls.

Twenty minutes later, Mommy walked out of the office with a large envelope in her hand. "Let's go," she said with a spring in her step.

From that day forward, our moving plans seemed to be on halt. I didn't want to think about co-signing on a place with my mom. I had put our new car in my name a few months ago and felt that was good enough. The thought of being in more debt made my stomach churn.

My focus was on saving for my future. I had just gotten a new job as an insurance agent and was scheduled to start training for work soon.

One morning, while I was completing a training exercise, my brother was on the phone with his friend. I don't recall how the topic about moving came up. But Jonathan saw me sitting at the dining room table and approached me.

"It's not fair. All that debt at this age," I bawled.

He couldn't empathize with me. "You're so dramatic. You're going to build history with the bank."

History or not, I didn't care. Debt was debt.

* * *

Several days later, I changed my mind. When I was walking home from work, I saw three police officers standing in our backyard, each carrying an assault rifle.

My first thought was, *Mom's home by herself.* With no man in the apartment to protect her, I wondered if she was okay and hurried inside.

I informed Mom about the police presence. She opened our sliding door blinds, and although she had been oblivious to the officers standing outside, the ruckus above started to make sense to her. "The new people have been flushing their toilet every hour."

"*Really?* That's weird."

And up until 9 p.m., they still were flushing it.

That was the last straw. It was the moment that told me we had to get out of Lysons Landing. I was going to co-sign, and yes, that meant more debt, but that didn't matter to me anymore. This was our sign that we had to go. And that's when our moving plans started to roll.

* * *

I got in touch with a realtor after scrolling through listings on Zolo. He was a young Eastern European fellow named Iwan. "All that matters to me is that my clients find a place they love," he'd say. "You guys are my favourite. Anything for you."

But moving wasn't the easiest process. Our two biggest obstacles were finding a place and getting a mortgage. At first, I went hunting for a townhouse. Mom always told me how much she had loved our home in Aurora, so I thought we should look for something similar.

For weeks, I searched for what we once had. The housing market in Mississauga and Oakville were above our price range. Our next best bet was Aurora and Caledon. But when Jonathan went with Iwan to see a property in Aurora, he decided against it. "It's not worth the price." And when all three of us went to Caledon to check out a duplex, we thought we were moving backwards, not forwards.

"It's Mississauga or Oakville," we agreed.

We started looking for condominiums, but even that was challenging. Everyone seemed to be interested in the same places we had been. I'd see a new condo listed on Zolo during a lecture and text Iwan that Mom would like it. Her taste in design was similar to mine. Then I'd leave class early to meet him at the spot.

Thereafter, we'd find ourselves in bidding war after bidding war. "Let's make an offer slightly below the asking price," Iwan would suggest. That was the smartest strategy. But each time we'd put in a proposal, someone would offer more than the asking price.

"Yikes!" I'd scream. I wanted to obtain a home and people were inflating the market, making it harder for folks to purchase properties in the future. There was no logic in it.

"I miss the days when homes were $200,000," Iwan would say. Things had changed.

In September, we made two offers on condos at Cedar Glendon, a complex with two-story units. We were beaten by a long shot on our first attempt at buying a property there. Someone had made an offer $30,000 above the asking price. I tried so hard not to cry as I talked to my mother that night.

"This one hurt," Mom said.

It did until I saw another listing pop up. This was our second chance. I wanted us to see the unit right away.

Much like the first condo, everything was upscale. The kitchen was spotless. The appliances were brand-new. The tiles were shiny. We saw ourselves making it our home.

Iwan stood at the top of the staircase. "The last property sold above the listed price."

I didn't want to believe that would happen again. "I'm sure we'll get it," I said.

"Let's make an offer," Mom announced.

Iwan nodded. "We should do it tonight."

We were the only bidders until someone had made an offer a couple of nights afterwards. I lowered my gaze to the ground upon hearing the news.

"There's no point in trying again, Milla," Mom said. "It's time to move on."

Pessimism overtook me. We had been condo hunting for months and nothing had come of it. Perhaps God didn't want us to move. Disgruntled, I went to bed.

From then on, my mom took the lead on the move. My preference was for the maintenance fee to be under $500. But there was a problem: it was getting closer to the end of the year, and there were fewer properties on the market.

Mom combed through the pages of listings. She pointed and said, "We should look at this one." It was the place I had been avoiding for weeks, the one with the high maintenance fee.

I was hesitant. The last thing I wanted was to move into a better place and struggle financially. I didn't know if we could handle a condo fee above $500. Mom was sure we could.

I wanted to respect my mother's decision. And yet, at the same time, I wanted to vocalize my apprehension to her about our potential buy. It was a hard position for me to find myself in.

When you're still a child but have been playing the role of the adult, confidant, and advisor, a power struggle can arise. Not only had I been supporting Mommy emotionally when her relationships with her mother and siblings deteriorated, but I had also taken the lead with the move. No one could argue that this big decision was just as much mine as it was my mother's, but I still had to obey the roles of the familial hierarchy. So, the fixer—me—had to fall back and let my mom guide us. Admittedly, releasing control was a scary thing for me to do.

"I'll go on the title deed by myself," Mom said.

I fought my urge to roll my eyes at her. *Why would she say that?*

"What do you want to do?" my mom asked.

I kept both hands on the steering wheel and turned my head towards her. "I never said I didn't want to co-sign. You have to choose which condo *you* want."

At the end of the day, it was my mom's decision to make. She was investing more into the new place than I was. All I wanted was for us to make a wise financial choice. The maintenance fee at 111 Transition Road was hefty, but if that's what Mom wanted, then so be it.

Iwan set up a day when we'd visit the condo. Mom and I wandered around inside. "It feels like home," I said. Mom got the same feeling as well. We had been longing to feel that vibe again. Like the good ole' days in Aurora.

That afternoon, when we arrived back at Lysons Landing, I realized that this whole time I had been searching for a home, and our home had been staring us in the face. It might not have been what I originally wanted, but it was certainly what we needed. The condo was across the street from my job, close to my university, and despite the location, it was quiet.

When it was all said and done, we chose the homelike unit with the glazed sandstone tiled round shower and glass door. Along with the white kitchen, the washroom was one of the most stunning parts about the condo. I couldn't wait to bathe in it.

No water leaking from the ceiling? *Check.* No mouldy walls? *Check.* No racing out of the stuffy restroom? *Check.*

This time, even with another bidder in the mix, we didn't have to fight to obtain it. December 19th was the day our lives would change.

I anticipated the joy that lay ahead. *"We have three weeks left … Now it's two weeks."*

The week before we moved, I made plans for each day so I'd be away from our apartment. I wanted to keep myself busy in order to make time feel like it was passing more quickly.

After exam season was done, I went to Toronto and saw Celine Dion in concert by myself. Then I went to Grandma's house in La Prairie. I wanted to tell her that we were moving, but we wanted only positive vibes for ourselves before we moved. Given the past, we didn't know if we'd get that from any of our relatives.

* * *

I woke up bright and early on moving day. There was a list of things I had to do before Mom came home from work. My goal was to make the day joyous for everyone. After all, it was our new beginning. A rosier one.

Outside, I threw out old items, school papers, and documents in the garbage and recycling bins. Coco, my best friend since high school, called her brothers Mark and Peter to help my brother and me discard our two worn-out couches.

"You carry the right side, and I'll carry the left," Jonathan instructed Mark.

"One … two … three," they shouted.

The next thing on our list was to get the rental truck. Mark and my brother rode in the rental. Peter and I drove in his dark green sedan.

I didn't trust the people in our neighbourhood. I wouldn't have been surprised if someone unlocked the rental truck, and ran off with our new mattresses and belongings. So we drove to the house of my close friend, Chloe, parked the truck in her driveway, and ate the most delicious meat lover's pizza.

When I got back home, I continued packing up our items in totes and cardboard boxes. Mom walked through the door an hour later. "You guys aren't done packing?"

I was hurt by her response. I had spent all day throwing things out and packing things up. That's what I felt she should've been focused on.

I pointed at an empty box. "Can you help put the plates in there?"

While Mommy and I wrapped newspapers around the plates, my father figure, Tony, arrived at our apartment. Since Louis and Mom had broken up, I called him instead. I knew Tony would show up for me. He and Jonathan lifted the heavy boxes and totes into the moving truck.

I glanced at the ticking clock and turned my head towards the guys. "Remember, we have to be at the condo by 8 p.m. Mom and I will drive behind you. Iwan will meet us there."

Mom and I were the last to arrive at the pristine looking front doors of the condominium. We hopped out of our car excited to move our stuff inside. But when we found my brother, he was pacing.

"What's wrong?"

"They won't let us bring our stuff inside," he said. "The security doesn't want to let us in."

I was upset. There was no reason for them not to allow us inside. As far as I was concerned, we were going to move our belongings in that night. I didn't care what anyone said.

Then I took a second to reflect and remembered how unpleasant the security guard was towards us. On every occasion we visited our new home, Palwinder would never greet me, my mother, or our agent Iwan. He could barely look us in the eye. *He's rude*, I thought.

Everyone agreed to take in whatever we could. As we brought in a few totes, the same security guard and his partner stopped us in our tracks. "You can't bring your items inside!"

"What are you talking about?" I asked them.

"The elevator has to be booked. The last reservation is at 7:30 p.m."

It was now past 8:30 p.m. To make matters worse, none of us knew the elevators had to be reserved beforehand, not even our agent.

"Our items aren't large," I said.

"You still can't come in," Palwinder replied. "I'll have you evicted!"

"Oh, please! I *own* my condo. We're going in," Mom replied.

That one word "own" hit Palwinder hard, his surprise apparent as he realized a Black woman owned a unit in the building. His assumption that we were renting and his belief that he could kick us out highlighted his prejudice.

It was hard to come to terms with the prevalence of prejudiced attitudes in Canada again. At sixteen, a white guy I had befriended at a McMaster summer school program called me the n-word on Facebook after I mentioned that I hadn't faced racism. This experience with Palwinder was another necessary wake-up call for me. Black Canadians can sometimes live in a bubble, shielded from the reality that even People of Colour hold discriminatory beliefs towards us here.

Whether it was hearing my six-foot-four-inch-tall brother explain why he wants to be more conscious of his stature to appear less intimidating after an elderly racially ambiguous woman clung to her purse upon seeing him on the bus, or witnessing a Black classmate make a joke with our Filipino high school substitute teacher who displayed a negative attitude by referring to Black students as "you people," the experience of being disliked for simply being beautifully melanated was evident. This is why I've never been a fan of the term *POC*.

As the Indian security guard saw it, that day, my brother was the aggressive Black man, I was the irate, rude Black girl, and my mother was the financially unstable Black woman who was unable to buy a property in her name. We weren't going to let his presumptions affect us, though. Palwinder could prohibit us from moving all of our belongings inside until the following day, but he had no choice but to let us enter our condo.

My heart ached. I worked hard to ensure our moving process was seamless and life was showing me that, yet again, I couldn't control everything.

"Mom, I feel like we're fought every time we try to

do something good in our lives," I said, fighting back tears.

Somehow, Mommy was able to find the light despite the dark cloud that tried to overshadow our ascent into our new chapter. She looked at me with a glimmer in her eyes and said, "Oh, Milla, don't let this ruin our big accomplishment. It's been a beautiful day."

After everything was said and done, Palwinder allowed us to bring in a few totes with essentials, but he refused to let us bring our mattresses inside. So we slept on the floor. Despite the beauty of the dark brown laminate flooring, it was rough.

All night, I tossed and turned. I wept while covering my mouth so that my mom wouldn't hear the sounds of my agony while she snored beside me. *You never know what people have gone through*, I told myself. *That's why those guards should've been nicer to us!*

I went back and forth between anger, sadness, and concern. I didn't want anyone to take the moving truck. We parked it on the side of Coco's street. She assured me that it wouldn't be towed. I feared that it would be, or that someone would unlock it.

When I woke up at daybreak, I decided that I didn't want to hold hostility towards the security guards. After all, we'd have to see them again. I also didn't want to give them that much power over the start of my experience at 111 Transition Road.

I greeted the head of security with a smile. He gave me until 4 p.m. to bring our items inside. Three hours later, when our toothbrushes, soap, clothes, mattresses, and pots and pans were in our unit, is when I'd feel the emotion I wanted to experience from the beginning—glee.

* * *

We spent our first Christmas at 111 Transition Road showing gratitude to the Creator for our biggest gift: our home. My mom decided to announce the good news to our relatives in two days. Everyone was to gather at Aunt Celeste's house then.

When we arrived at Celeste's, we sat around the dining room table. My brother and I placed our butts between our chipper grandmother. "Bibi, can you say grace?"

As Mom closed her eyes and bent her head, everyone grabbed each other's hands. "I would like to thank God for helping us get a new place.

Grandma squeezed my hand. That small action told me that she was relieved. My grandma had always been a stoic woman throughout my life, but seeing her watery eyes and feeling the firmness in her touch told me that her heart was at peace, and that maybe she was sorry for everything in the past. She, along with Mommy, Jonathan, and me, could finally rest our heads now that we had said farewell to our last.

Fifteen

MY PURSUIT OF HAPPINESS

Self-awareness doesn't stop you from making mistakes;
it allows you to learn from them.

— Unknown

At 7 a.m., I stepped outside and turned my face away from the biting wind. *"Ow!"* I cried, standing near the traffic light. It was January 2020, one of the coldest winters in a long time.

As I crossed the main street, an awareness hit me. I recognized an imbalance orbiting throughout my life. Mom and Jonathan both had cars. They could get to work and school faster. That was a relief. Yet here I was, trudging through snow that felt like it was up to my knees.

I waited at the Miway bus stop, hoping to see bus 2E approaching. Fifteen minutes passed and still no bus. This was the third time in three weeks that the bus had failed to show up.

Why is my life this way? I asked myself as I walked to the nearest bus station. That question sounded ungrateful to me. We had just moved into a new place. I had gotten everything that I'd asked for. *Don't think that way. Things will work out in your favour someday.*

But that frigid morning when I almost missed class wouldn't be the last time I'd feel this type of pain. This was only the beginning to an end of this inequality I had felt since youth.

* * *

In October my energy had been different. It was low, the lowest it had been in a while. I felt like I was on the verge of a depression.

By November, I was tired of walking around my condo pretending to be okay. *No more excuses*, I told myself. I had to get to the root of this prolonging feeling.

I bent forward and lay face down on my purple floral yoga mat. On the surface, I was aware that I felt disillusionment, insecurity, and uncertainty. Some of my discomfort was due to there being an upcoming transition in my life. I was in my final year of university and watching my peers apply for master's degrees. The pressure to follow the same route was getting to me. But I hadn't yet decided what I wanted to do professionally.

A career in psychotherapy was what I chose. I had always been intrigued by people, their way of thinking and behaving. I wanted to learn about the inner workings of the brain. Besides that, being a psychotherapist would allow me to help people, and I thought I'd be successful in it.

There were two obstacles: my GPA wasn't where it needed to be, and I didn't have enough volunteer experience. I had struggled throughout my studies due to life's challenges and laziness. It also didn't help that the biology degree I had initially chosen didn't inspire me. I was good at science, and my mother had encouraged me to pursue a career in healthcare when I was in high school. "We'll always need doctors," she'd say. "Healthcare isn't going anywhere."

Regardless of how true those statements were, I released myself from my mom's expectations and changed my major from biology to psychology. But I ran into another problem: I hadn't interacted with any of my professors before or after I had switched my major, and now I needed references. My blood pressure rose.

My favourite psychology professor and the manager at a Salvation Army church where I had volunteered since my youth vouched for me, which was a relief. However, upon reflection, my uncertainty throughout this process should have been a clear indication that I wasn't aligned with my life's purpose. I understood the task: to help people. But not feeling calm and at peace about my decision to become a psychotherapist was my sign that the job wasn't meant for me.

One of the biggest goals I had for myself since I was an adolescent was to pay off my student loan debt before I graduated in June 2021. My inability to do so was something else that disappointed me. I had worked so much over the years and could have paid off my debt, but I had other financial responsibilities to take care of. To make matters worse, I had lost my job that summer. I was content to take a break from working. The only cons were not being able to save and pay off loans. For years, I had feared being in debt and messing up my credit. Witnessing what my mother went through after our time in Caledon weighed on my mind recurrently.

Then there was my love life, or lack thereof. There wasn't much activity happening in the love department, and when there was, it wasn't what my heart desired. I'd frequently find myself in situations where guys weren't courageous enough to approach me, or I'd deal with silly games from immature guys who I wasn't interested in. I just couldn't understand why it was hard for me to find a genuinely nice guy, someone who was on my level. Even back then, I didn't want to settle. So I was willing to accept a life by myself if I wasn't going to get my wish fulfillment.

The real honesty and breakthrough occurred within me when I finally acknowledged that, for most of my life, there had been an imbalance. At first, it was hard for me to admit that truth. But it was important for me to confess to myself that I had often prioritized my mother and brother over myself, and as I saw it, the same level of reciprocity was not always present.

When Mom wanted me to buy items for her every once in a while, I would be called mean if I hesitated. I'd often give in, even if I was short on change, and regardless of whether my mom was joking when she'd call me mean. The word *mean*, though, had stuck with me for years, and so did the feeling of being unappreciated.

Now, I had stopped arguing with my spirit. I gave permission to myself to tell *my* truth.

I had also accepted a heavy feeling that existed within me: my mom had favoured my brother in some way too. Whenever we'd get into our heated arguments, she would take his side. I was left being told that I was at fault, indirectly and directly, or that I was mean.

I was tired of that. I was tired of no one choosing me. So I chose myself.

"What will make you happy?" was my next question. My answer was simple: I want to focus on myself. And I didn't want to feel guilty about it.

I did.

Mom had to be taken care of before I could start my life. Knowing that she was okay would put me at ease. That's the only way I could have peace. Then I could do whatever I pleased.

In spite of that feeling, I knew it was necessary for me to be specific with what my soul's desires were. Taking care of Mom was great. But what did I want?

Three beautiful children. Deep inside, I still hoped to find a proper life partner. I owed my children the experience of having a father. I didn't want them to suffer the way that I had.

A house, a reliable car ... I want to give back to people. Thinking about monetarily helping strangers, especially Black single mothers and Congolese people, made my face glow. It would provide me with incalculable fulfillment.

Most of all, I wanted to pay off my student loan debt and live a harmonious life. That was it. A simple, fulfilling, peaceful life. And I was going to attain that by focusing on myself.

But after all this internal dialogue, a part of me felt depleted, as if I were too weak, almost fragile. I was trapped in my situation, and although I could see the light, I couldn't completely find my way out.

What would focusing on myself actually entail? It started with looking deeply within myself. I had to acknowledge my shadow traits, the "bad" ones that had been overlooked. It was time that I approached myself in an honest, loving, and caring way. That's how I'd create healing, and eventually, the life I wanted.

Once I understood this, an event from a month ago popped into my mind. I was on the phone with my friend Estella, eating Cajun shrimp and fries. Jonathan approached my room, and we started our sibling banter.

I looked at him and said, "Put some lotion on your ashy hands!"

"*Ouch*," Estella said. "Wasn't there a better way to say that?"

My answer was prideful. "No."

Even though the way my words came out didn't sound harsh from my point of view, the truth is I could have conveyed my message better. I hadn't intended for my tone to be sharp, but that's how it was perceived by my friend, brother, and mother. So, I acknowledged that I can be abrasive.

To fix this behaviour, I'd challenge myself. When I'd wake up in the morning, I would complete mundane tasks: brush my teeth, wash my face, do my hair, and change. But I noticed that rushing through those activities contributed to my stress and impatience. I was behaving as if I were in a race against time. So, I slowed down my morning routine by practicing breathing techniques and meditating before interacting with my family at the start of each day.

I'd also examine my abrasiveness and impatience with my mother and brother. My responses, along with my internal dialogue were graded every day. *You did a good job, but you could've done better,* I'd tell myself. *Let's work on being more patient tomorrow.*

Then I pinpointed the times in my life where I had displayed unkindness. In elementary school, a classmate of mine gravitated towards me. I wasn't receptive to her, though, and thought creating distance would make her get the hint. It didn't.

This memory stuck out to me because, even as a child, I had great awareness. You never know what someone else is going through, so I always wanted to show people kindness.

Years after my classmate and her twin sister moved, I found out that they were foster kids. Hearing that brought tears to my eyes, and I regretted not befriending her. Looking back on this now, irrespective of the fact that I didn't have to befriend my classmate if I didn't feel a connection with her, I recognize that I could've navigated my relationship with her better.

I showed similar behaviour towards another classmate in high school. I attributed my need to distance myself from her because of my irritability from living in Lysons Landing. I was on edge every day because of the banging and stomping above my head, so the smallest nuances in my environment could upset me.

Tally never did anything wrong. She was nice and generous. But I started getting annoyed with her during math class. Most of the time, it was because she'd ask me to clarify what the teacher was saying when I'd be just as confused as everyone else. Another time, it was because she asked to use my calculator.

"This is the last time," I snapped, handing her the calculator.

She stared at me, taken aback. "I don't know what I ever did to you." I've since been able to apologize to her for my harsh tone.

The last situation I thought about involved my elementary school crush Trey. Before recess, he walked to my cubby and called my name.

I caught an attitude. "What!"

"Do you want to be my girlfriend?"

I was upset for two reasons: he had taken three years to tell me that he liked me, and I felt that he had asked me out because I liked another boy.

"No, I'll never be your girlfriend!"

"You're so mean," he replied with a soft smile.

I didn't deserve that grin. I now see how horrible my reaction to Trey was, and have since apologized to him, too.

What this was all truly about, I understand more clearly as I get older. It has been my experience that people reveal things about us. When revelations come through life events and feedback from people, you should reflect on what's happened and what's being said, especially if there are recurrences. Repetition is the universe's way of telling us to pay attention. If we don't, we'll continue to go through similar experiences until we get the lesson.

Something clicked within me when I recalled Estella's remark about my harsh words towards my brother. It prompted me to reflect on my own behaviour and acknowledge the negative aspects of my personality so that I could learn to control my less favourable traits better.

The first step in ensuring that I didn't fall back into past versions of myself I no longer aligned with, was acknowledging negative behavioural patterns so that I could replace them with newer, healthier ones. Challenging myself daily was the last step. That was the ultimate test.

I've been successful ever since I implemented these techniques in my life. It's not to say that I still don't have missteps. I'm a flawed human being, and both my good and bad traits are forever a part of me, so I'll continue to make mistakes. But sitting down with myself and looking at my darkness has enabled me to evolve.

This chart was made with encouragement from the *To My Sisters* podcast. It helped me identify my stronger and weaker traits, along with the ones that I'm still working on. I believe it's important for everyone to recognize the lightness and darkness inside of them. Doing so, will enable us to show up in this world being more authentic, balanced, and hopefully, lighter people. *Ascension* is the ultimate goal.

5 Light Traits	5 Shadow Traits
1. Kind	1. Cold
2. Gentle/Warm	2. Abrasive
3. Calm	3. Impaient/Impulsive
4. Giving	4. Prideful
5. Understanding	5. Judgemental

Sixteen

L'AMOUR DE SOI

The longest relationship you'll have with someone is yourself, so learn to love the beauty that exists within and outside of you.

— Jamilla Kabongo-Bah

My whole life I've been surrounded by society's beauty standards, the standards I don't conform with due to my hue. At Parkdale Public School, Bailey, a blue eyed, dirty blonde-haired classmate of mine, and Taylor did. They were the two girls I admired the most.

Bailey was in my grade two class. We had different friend groups and barely talked. I'd secretly dote on her beauty from afar. *She's pretty*, I thought.

Taylor and I were close. She was three years my senior but would hang out with her friends and me during recess. One of those friends was a guy named Jack. Whenever I was around Taylor, he'd be there, vying for her attention.

I found Taylor beautiful for the most simple and odd thing: the large scar across her olive-skinned cheek. It was unique. On top of Taylor's natural beauty, she was humble and kind. Being pretty and nice made her the total package in my eyes. I wanted to be like her when I grew up.

At eight years old, I didn't think I was unattractive. I wondered if people thought I was, particularly Jack and later a guy named, Timmy, who I met at summer camp. They were both white. I was younger than them and Black.

Would Timmy find me attractive? I wondered. *Does he like Black girls?* These questions would persist in my mind as I grew older, just like they do in other Black girls. The sad part is that it takes us a while to understand that they have less to do with who we think we are and more to do with what Western society falsely says we are: unpretty, unworthy, and undesirable.

Oh, how I wish we'd stop believing that.

* * *

Puberty is an awkward transitioning stage for most people, the phase where we go from being a young girl or boy to a woman or man. Menstrual cycles, growth spurts, pubic hair, sweating, and growing breasts. I didn't like it.

I had moved to Mississauga when this chapter of my life started. Living in that city was a big adjustment for me. At the schools I went to in Caledon, I was surrounded by Black and brown people. Now that I found myself attending Eastwood Public School in Mississauga, I no longer did. I was around all walks of life. I loved it. But I went from being around Black boys who doted on Black girls to being around ones who were interested in anything but Black girls.

Seeing Black boys fawn over white girls with "big butts" when that was something Black women were made fun of for centuries was upsetting. The body part that was used to humiliate and weaponize Black women such as Sarah Baartman, whose body had been put on display in "freak show attractions" for 19th century Europeans to gaze at, was now the very thing that boys in the Black community were praising on all ethnicities but their own. It was troubling and confusing. *Her butt isn't even big,* I'd tell myself. And yet, they still drooled over it.

Mom and I would have the derriere discussion over the years. "It wasn't until a white, curvaceous Latina became popular that big butts were accepted by white people," she'd say. Mommy would look at herself in the mirror. "But Beyoncé helped me celebrate mine."

Before modern influential celebrities like Queen Bey appeared in the music industry, there weren't many Black women with so-called stereotypical features who were celebrated. Black women were, and still are, forced to uplift ourselves while living in a society that celebrates our features: large butts, curves, full lips, curly hair, and dark skin on everyone else but ourselves.

* * *

I'd receive the opposite treatment, too: being surrounded by perverted guys. The young boys who'd brazenly stare at your chest and the older men who'd shamelessly hound you. Finding myself in either situation was discomforting.

My breasts first began to grow when I was ten years old. I feared that my boobs would make me the centre of attention. They were visible now.

One evening at PLASP, Elijah, a six-year-old boy, pointed at me. "What are those?" I shuffled my *Pokémon* card deck, hoping he'd drop his question, but his eyes were stuck on mine.

"What do you mean?"

He touched my chest. "*Those!*"

I had hoped, perhaps foolishly in retrospect, that no one would point out my growing breasts. I disliked them. They made me just as uncomfortable as I was when Elijah had grazed them.

In middle school, it seemed like I went from a B cup size to a D overnight. There was no way that my boobs wouldn't be noticeable. The guys in my neighbourhood and at Eastwood Public School would make googly eyes at them depending on what I wore. So I'd cover the top of my body with big sweaters. They hid my breasts and chubbiness, the lower belly I could never get rid of. And I'd wear loose pants to mask the cellulite on my legs. I presumed that wearing baggy clothes would minimize male attention.

One day, on my way home after school, I decided to take a shortcut. As I was walking, a middle-aged Black man in a pickup truck stopped and honked at me.

I've always had a fear of being taken advantage of. I think most women do. So my shoulders jumped when I saw him. *Act like you don't see him*, I told myself. I held my head down, turned in the opposite direction where there was a crowd of people, and took a different route home.

Months later is when I'd take the shortcut again. *You can't live in fear*. As a woman, sometimes that's hard to do.

* * *

Things changed when I entered high school. I enjoyed receiving attention from guys. Now I'm sure that barely getting male gaze in middle school contributed to that switch. That, along with not being positively affirmed at home, especially by a father. Physically and emotionally present fathers teach their daughters how to be loved, cherished, and treated by a man. In turn, they do not seek male validation, and their self-esteem remains stable.

I liked getting attention from attractive guys without trying. It made me feel pretty and wanted. But when I didn't have eyes on me, I'd demonstrate an unhealthy pattern: assisting guys in approaching me. When I'd heard from a mutual friend that my crush and later boyfriend, David, was attracted to me, I got David's number and immediately texted him. I chased him.

Worse than that, sometimes I'd make minor interactions with men I'd meet during outings or on campus at university seem more significant than they were in reality. I'd interpret someone's kindness as a sign that they liked me. I'd even emotionally attach myself to some men during a state of limerence. Then I'd be the one hurt or feeling insecure when my feelings weren't reciprocated.

* * *

Male gaze concerned me just as much as my hair and glasses. For as long as I can remember, I've been dissatisfied with my hair length. I wished my hair was longer.

The concentration on my hair began in my childhood and followed me until I was twenty-three years old. I'd watch my family friend, Mary, getting her hair braided when we lived on Bellarosa Lane. She would sob during the detangling process. I sat with my mouth open, in awe of the length of her hair. Secretly, I wished my hair could be long like hers.

In high school and university, I'd mask this insecurity by wearing a weave. It was the best solution. I could appear to have longer hair while my real hair grew underneath. That worked until some of my Black girl peers noticed the difference in my hair texture.

"Is that your real hair?" someone would ask.

My answer was simple, short, and filled with pride. "Yes."

I disliked being asked that question. As I saw it, the weave tracks were on my head, so it was my hair. It also wasn't anyone's business.

As Black people, especially women, we have an unhealthy obsession with our hair. While colonialism and Western society imposed this fixation onto us, we continue to perpetuate it. Every time our mothers, grandmothers, and aunts took us to the hair salon to straighten our hair or fried our hair with a hot comb before a special event, we were being told that our curls, whether tight or loose, and "kinky" were and are less than.

It's not. Our hair is beautiful, delicate, and presentable. All it requires is love, patience, and nourishment.

That's the thing I didn't understand. Mom would tell me that I must have a healthy relationship with my hair. I'd brush her words off. But when I started to accept and love my hair, it grew without much effort. Simply finding beauty within allowed me to foster adoration for my external self because everything is connected. Mind, body, soul, and spirit.

To be clear: my hair length and its texture never determined my beauty. My value as a woman doesn't change whether my hair is two or twelve inches long. The hair we have is meant to be an extension of who we are, not what we are.

Then there were my glasses. The large specs I'd been forced to wear since I was four years old because of my lazy eye, a trait that I got from my father. Wearing them has been my longest insecurity. As much as they've become a part of who I am, at times I wished they weren't a part of my identity.

I was teased by my childhood crush, Trey, and my other peers. "How many fingers am I holding up?" he'd ask.

I'd cross my arms and kiss my teeth. "Five!"

There wasn't much of an alternative for me until I became of age to start wearing contacts. I'd only wear them during special events when I wanted to look "prettier." In all honesty, I'm still working on getting rid of the belief that I'm more beautiful without my glasses.

* * *

Pretty privilege has been a heavily debated topic within more recent years. To some people, I am pretty, and to others, I am not. I accept that, as should you. Knowing that we're not meant for everyone, and everyone isn't meant for us will put you at ease. It's given me peace.

Being "pretty" isn't all that people think it's cracked up to be. It often comes with jealousy, envy, betrayal, and gossip. These are all things I've experienced through-out my first twenty-six years of life.

My first introduction to what female jealousy looked like was in grade four. Tae was a gorgeous, dark-skinned classmate of mine. She always wore her long black hair in a ponytail.

Wow! I thought. *Another Black girl with long hair.*

On a sunny day, before we were let outside for recess, Tae sat next to me and said, "Well, I want to tell Trey that I like him." She rolled her eyes. "But he likes you."

I got up from my seat. For one, it wasn't her place to tell me that Trey liked me. If he couldn't tell me that himself, then no one else should have. I also couldn't control who was seeking my affection. From my per-spective, there was no reason for the bad energy.

I'd find myself in similar situations thereafter, or worse. I've dealt with girls who've betrayed our friend-ship by talking to a guy I was interested in, completely disregarding my feelings. The one that still makes me chuckle is being told not to be the person who upstages the birthday girl.

I understood that I was dealing with the projection of other women's insecurities, but that didn't make the blows hurt less. Every situation disheartened me in some way.

Thankfully, Mommy and I had each other to lean on. "Milla, the girls at work were talking about my pants," she'd say. "They were looking at my butt in them."

I could sense the pain in her voice and tried to lift her up in those moments. "Mommy, don't worry. It's not about you. It's about them."

I meant every word. My mom is a beautiful woman and her beauty, inwardly and outwardly, threatens some women. It isn't her fault. Just like it isn't mine or yours.

Mom would encourage me, too. One day, I confided in her about the size of my lips. "When I was younger, I didn't like them." Mom's response has stuck with me ever since. *"Girl, people pay for those lips!"* I laugh at that retort whenever it comes to mind. It's gold!

While I understand that many people don't care to hear "pretty" girls' grievances, that doesn't mean that we don't have them. With anything in life, there are pros and cons. I can admit that my charm has helped propel me in different areas of my life, even so, that doesn't mean that I haven't also suffered due to that same charm. All women's voices deserve to be heard.

* * *

Now, don't get me wrong, I've always had some level of confidence. I've purposely carried myself a certain way. I know that my pride had a lot to do with that (and still does). I just refused to uncloak myself. The truth is that I do have insecurities, and I'm working on them daily.

Learning to uplift myself has been hard. But every morning that I'm blessed to see another glorious day, I look at my reflection in my bathroom mirror and read out the positive affirmations on yellow sticky notes I made for myself. They help me see my inner and outer beauty. I'm a firm believer that the more you say something, the more you'll believe it and that it will become true. The power of manifestation is limitless.

I am abundant. I am beautiful. I am confident. I am worthy. I am valuable. I am deserving. Understand and know that I am deserving and worthy of great things. I am the ultimate catch, as are you. I love me. And when you truly love yourself, your true essence, you will know just how much of a prize you are. No one else will ever be able to tell you otherwise because your real beauty comes from *within*.

Seventeen

CHILDHOOD WOUND

Life is but a mirror looking back at us, uncovering the layers we've neglected to see.

— Unknown

$\mathcal{B}$*oom. Boom. Boom.* That was the sound of Auntie Felicia thumping down the oak staircase in the family house in Caledon to confront Uncle Luke. *Crash!* was the noise of the glass cup shattering on the kitchen floor when my grandmother threw it at my mother in front of my tender eleven-year-old eyes. *"Tu es stupide!"* were the words Grandma shouted at Mommy when Sharon, the astute police officer, came to our front door to question us about a disturbance.

These memories had been replaying in my mind since November of 2020. *That was some messed up shit!* I'd tell myself as each memory resurfaced. Then I'd throw the old film tapes back into the storage compartment inside my head.

But those "forgotten" old films hadn't been playing without reason. No matter how many times I pressed the pause button, hoping the memories of my past would fade to black and disappear forever, the universe kept trying to tell me something. It was time for me to start healing from my childhood wounds.

* * *

The week after my twenty-third birthday, I sat on my bed and let one particular memory play from beginning to end. As I remembered seeing my mom standing inches away from the broken glass that almost struck her body, I got the shivers. That night, she could have been seriously injured. But even if Mom hadn't obtained any external scars (and thank God for that), she, my brother, and I had acquired internal ones.

Overcome with grief, one morning, I walked towards the kitchen. I looked at my mom with damp eyes and said, "Mom, I don't know how you did it."

"Did what?" she responded, washing the dishes.

"Showed … immeasurable bravery, strength, and grace towards people who didn't deserve it." I didn't have to name who. My mother's silent nod, wrinkled nose, and lowered eyebrows—the look she gets when she's trying to hide her pain—told me she knew I was not only talking about Grandma but also our other relatives. They all had become upset with the physical distance and lack of communication that developed between us and them a year after we moved to 111 Transition Road.

Soon after my conversation with my mom, I felt the urge to talk to my younger but often wiser brother, who was twenty-one at the time. Out of everyone in my life, Jonathan was the only person who could understand the depth of my grief. We were the children who had seen everything: the aggression, abandonment, mistreatment, and verbal and physical violence.

After Papa appeared in my mom's dreams weeks before Auntie Celeste's wedding in 2010, Mom had continued to encourage us to show grace towards our relatives. That's what we did every time we'd arrive at family events in high spirits while suppressing our childhood pain.

But I'd grown tired of participating in the tight-knit family facade. Desperate for life-changing advice, I turned to my brother, who had stopped attending family events after his sixteenth birthday. "How did you heal from what we went through when we were children?"

He paused for a moment as we drove in his black Honda Civic and then glanced over at me. "Let's talk about it at the lake." Rap music shook the car and momentarily silenced the voice in my head.

We parked at the frozen lake around Port Credit and sat in his car. Jonathan turned the ignition off. Then he took a deep breath and said, "I wrote. That's what helped me when I was younger." My brother waved his long index finger in my direction. "You need to write, Jamilla!"

His advice was a sign. A *higher* sign. One that I saw as clearly as the blue sky.

A few days later, I wrote in a purple Michael Jackson notebook I'd bought at the Bramalea City Centre during the time when we had been commuting from Toronto to Brampton and Caledon, and back and forth. Since then, I'd never used it. But during the following days, which turned into months, that notebook became my most trusted confidant.

I'd express my emotions about whatever I felt, especially the baggage I'd been carrying subconsciously. Feeling angry about being physically punished by my mom for "swearing" when I was six years old. Feeling sad about being kicked out of our house in Caledon and becoming homeless. Or feeling happy about something simple: the beautiful walk I'd taken around the lake near my condo.

There are almost a dozen notebooks that have ink in them because of me now.

* * *

My last final for university was completed in the spring of 2021. We were still on lock down, a time I admittedly enjoyed because I've always been a homebody, but also because it made me and everybody slow down our lives. It gave us time to breathe, think, and reflect. Without the lockdown, I don't know if I could have successfully begun my healing journey. *I needed it.*

But there was a downside. Many people lost their lives during the pandemic, especially the older population. They were treated as if they didn't matter, something I didn't understand or like. Regardless of the state of the world and one's age, decent healthcare should be accessible to everyone. It's a basic human right. And being away from people, even loved ones, affected our mental health and social skills.

Witnessing these negative effects only intensified my desire to be a listening ear for people struggling with life. Still, I had no clarity on how I should pursue this passion professionally. So, I applied to retail jobs instead, and remained dedicated to my internal growth and healing journey.

Focusing on myself would change when I could no longer shake off my nagging intuition that kept saying, *Write a book, Jamilla.* As far as I was concerned, I had no story to tell.

Despite my lack of belief, I woke up one day and decided to listen to that inner voice. While I sat on my desk chair and made notes about my life in a Word document, I soon realized that I had an interesting life story to share with people, and the Caledon chapters only scratched the surface of it. My first childhood wound wasn't formed during the time I lived there.

I might have only had bits and pieces of the puzzle, but I knew one thing: my story hadn't started in Aurora like I had thought up until I was nine years old. I was born in England and was raised by two parents until I wasn't. So, what really happened there? What was my mother's story?

I wanted to know the full truth, so I went searching for answers.

THE STORY

The womb of the woman is the most sacred place on Earth.

— African proverb

"Mom, I've been keeping a secret," I said. "I've been writing a book. I need your help filling in the missing pieces."

She smiled. "I knew it!"

I had been locking myself in my room since May. Mommy would crack the door open and see me typing away.

"*What's the full story?*"

"Milla, sit down and listen closely."

* * *

In 1998, at 12:01 p.m. in Wembley, London, a baby was born on a sun-beaming, winter afternoon. "The baby's name will be Jamilla or Jamal," my father told my mom before this day. *Jamilla* it was.

Mommy described me in the womb as an almost motionless fetus in the last months leading up to the day I was born. My lack of movement worried her, so she made an appointment with her OB-GYN.

"The baby is doing just fine, Sandra," Lily assured my mother with a heavy cockney accent. "She's *quiet*. But she's fine."

Despite my innate placid nature, a lot of tumultuous events would occur before and throughout my gestation period that indirectly and directly impacted me. For starters, my mom was going to have her first child at the delicate age of twenty. As the first-born daughter from a once well-off and proud Congolese family who had to abruptly leave their homeland, that was unacceptable.

Civil turmoil in the Democratic Republic of Congo, known from 1971 to 1997 as Zaire, began in the early 1990s when soldiers turned into dissenters under President Mobutu SeSe Seko's regime. "Où est l'argent?" Katangan troops demanded. President Mobutu, notorious for loading his pockets with money, didn't have compensation for his soldiers. The troops snapped.

Bang! Bang! Bang! Rebels fired their guns and vandalized streets a short distance from my mother's school. They were searching areas for anyone of Kasai origin living in the province of Katanga. They wanted foreigners, like my family, to leave permanently.

"Tout le monde, allons-y!" the teacher screamed, ushering students out of my mother's classroom.

Outside, my mom smelled the strong, sharp scent of gunpowder. Her eyes drifted back to her school. Then to the local stores, warehouses, and homes that had been looted. And the broken windows that left shattered glass on the ground. The city she called home was unrecognizable.

Somehow, my mom and her siblings made it home without a scratch. Someone—a friend, stranger, or bystander—drove them to their family house. But after my great-uncle Lucien found out the house phone had been tapped, they couldn't stay there for long.

"The family is being targeted. For your safety, you have to leave," he told them. Uncle Lucien arranged for the children to stay with Genevieve and Gabriel, a French couple who were friends of the family, until Papa returned from his business trip in Europe and Maman from her visit to South Africa.

My mom and her four siblings: Luke, Celeste, Felicia, and Rick hid somewhere in the couple's house while rebels scoured the town for targets. Only when the time was right, the children were snuck out of the home and spirited away in a black, tinted pickup van to the closest Zairean international airport. A private jet, owned by my grandfather's rich, white South African friend, awaited them. They were flown to Johannesburg, where my grandmother met them.

"Salut, mes enfants," she said, embracing them tightly.

By 1994, there was no way my family could turn back. When ethnic tensions between the Hutus and Tutsis deepened, Zaire was plunged into their civil war, exacerbating my people's distress. President Mobutu was pressured by his American and European "allies" to take in residents from our neighbouring country, Rwanda. But the Hutus, who were being massacred by the Rwandan Patriotic Front, came en masse. Due to concern that the Rwandan genocide would destabilize our land, Mobutu and the UN Refugee Agency agreed to repatriate refugees.

But in October 1996, Zaire was invaded by Rwanda under the pretense that the Hutu refugees who fled into my country posed a threat to Rwandan security. Congo, mon beau pays, has been in a constant state of civil war ever since. And, to this day, my people are violated through rape, torture, and seizing of ancestral land that is rich in natural resources such as coltan (used to make rechargeable batteries in phones, computers, and electric cars), cobalt, cassiterite, diamonds, lithium, and uranium by the country we gave a lending hand to.

While the family stayed in Johannesburg, Grandpa continued working as the director of La Gecamine Kolwezi, a Congolese mining company, until it became defunct. Through his work, he met a man from London, England. Papa decided that the family would emigrate.

After the horror they'd gone through, they hoped to rebuild their lives in Wembley. For my mother, a refugee turned modern African woman, the way forward seemed simple: obtain a higher education, engage in hypergamy, purchase a large home and a car, and then have children.

Having a baby, now, was the furthest thing on her mind.

* * *

Mom, a curvy, almond-skinned woman, dressed in a pair of black tights, a red blouse, and a sleek chignon, went for a trip to the nearest beauty supply store. As she waited on the platform of the transit station, she caught the eye of a slim, brown-skinned man. He approached her and struck up a conversation.

"Where are you from?" he asked her as they hopped onto the train and found seats.

"The Democratic Republic of Congo," Mommy replied.

"No way! I'm from Sierra Leone and Guinea Conakry."

Her ears perked up. My mom had never heard of the country Sierra Leone before now. She was intrigued.

"Here's my number. Call me any time," he told her. My mother slipped the scrap of paper into her handbag. She'd never call him.

A few evenings later, my mom and grandmother boarded the local bus together on their way home. Down the aisle, Mommy noticed the guy she had met on her first trip on the train. Her dark brown eyes locked on his. She got up and sat down beside him.

"You never called me," Marcus said, his voice riddled with disappointment.

"Sorry," my mom replied. "I was busy."

Much like their first interaction, there was a palpable synergy. Mom loosened up in Marcus' charming presence.

Their shared commonalities, being African and trying to find a way to rebuild their lives in the country known to offer people abundant opportunies, England, made it easy. Even so, she thought nothing of their chats. Marcus was just a new friend who also happened to live close by. Someone to talk to. And it didn't hurt that she found him attractive.

"Who was that?" Grandma asked when they arrived home.

"A guy I met the other day," Mom said. "He's from Sierra Leone and Guinea Conakry."

"Well … I don't like him."

To my grandma, who's always had a good eye for nice garments and accessories, first impressions mattered. Marcus was wearing a plain, blue t-shirt, Levi jeans, and sneakers. Right away, she assumed he wasn't a good fit for her daughter. Maybe she didn't know, or care, that casual attire was perfectly acceptable in the West; people dressed up or down regardless of wealth. Where my grandma came from, wealth came in a suit and tie. Her daughter had to marry a qualified admirer who could provide for her, and restore stability and honour to the family name. Not someone whose clothes signified a lack of sophistication. Low class.

"You have to look put together," she would say. "One must look proper." That's the Congolese way of life. The Congolese Sapeur.

It's a mindset my grandma would carry throughout her life and pass on to me. And it's an outlook I will inevitably hand off to my own children. Now, hopefully, with the gumption to not be so quick to judge a book by its cover, but also with great pride, too.

Grandma ordered communication between the two to cease. It didn't. Mommy and Marcus remained in contact without my grandmother, or anyone else in the family, knowing.

Initially, it was all innocent. They got to know each other more. Marcus would invite my mother to his apartment and cook traditional stews with cassava leaves and meat. The aroma from the peanut sauce mixed in the brewing pot pervaded every room, while the smoky-sweet voice of Beres Hammond played in the background.

Before they knew it, their growing friendship became romantic. Marcus' closest family and friends knew about his romance. My mom, on the other hand, kept her new beau a secret.

But one person wasn't so easily fooled. Mom's father, a hazel-eyed, statuesque man, observed that she was out a lot more than usual. Something or someone was preoccupying his daughter's attention.

"Is Sandra seeing anyone?" Papa asked my grandma.

"No, Bibi would tell me if she was," Grandma replied confidently. After all, they were close, as close as any mother and daughter could be.

* * *

"She's going to kill me!" Mom shouted.

"You're twenty years old," the nurse told her. "It's *your* decision to make."

Despite fear, my mom knew she had to tell her mother the truth. She could only hide her growing stomach for so long. And she desperately wanted reassurance from the woman who had birthed her that everything would be okay.

She found her mother in the kitchen, cooking. "Maman, I need to speak to you. It's *important.*"

My grandma led the way to the room my mom and her sister Celeste shared. "What's going on, Bibi?" Grandma asked, concerned.

Mom sat on the bed while my grandma stood over

her. "I'm ..." she said, exhaling deeply. "Pregnant."

"What? I can't believe it!" my grandmother exclaimed. "By whom?"

"The guy you saw me talking to on the bus."

Grandma's face was sallow. That was the guy she'd demanded Sandra to stop speaking to. The one, out of all of her daughter's strongest suitors, she couldn't stand.

"If you want to continue living with me and your father, get an abortion. If you want to keep the child, you must leave this house."

Mom's stomach twisted. This was the last thing she thought her mother, the woman who strode past a Katangan rebel uprising in 1978 while pregnant with her, the woman she looked up to and respectfully obeyed, the nurse of her family and the community, the matriarch, would say.

"I can't get an abortion," my mom told her.

As a young girl, my mother had seen her Aunt Claudette become a shell of a person as she struggled to conceive a child after her fallopian tubes were damaged during one of many abortion procedures. Mom didn't want to live with guilt or regret. Or worse than that—allow her sorrows to drive her to the bottle like Aunt Claudette. Grandma was incensed.

My mom ran to my father's apartment and informed him about my grandmother's request. He was excited about the pregnancy from the moment he found out, and so were his family members. That's the good news. I was *chosen* and *wanted* by both my mother and father.

* * *

When my mom returned to her cashier job at Flower Shop, her coworker Pamela, who also happened to be a friend of the family, took her to the side. "Your mom is distraught about the baby," Pamela said, creasing her forehead. "We should have a sit down at my house soon."

To preserve the solid foundation that held the family nest together, my parents agreed to attend. When they arrived, no pleasantries were exchanged. My father stretched out his hand, but Grandma refused to shake it. The discussion immediately commenced.

"Monsieur, I don't approve of your relationship with my daughter. You're not the right man for her," my grandmother declared. "I don't believe you'll be able to financially support my daughter and the baby."

The room was still. "You should get an abortion!" she said, looking at my mom.

Dad respectfully interjected. "My family and I don't want to get an abortion. We're okay with raising the child."

My grandma had nothing more to say. Neither did my parents. So, they left Pamela's house.

Mommy packed up her belongings and moved in with my dad and his roommate PJ not long afterwards. Being unwanted by her mother was an unfamiliar feeling. It stung. But at least she had a place to stay.

Grandma was gutted. She went into the backyard and cried for hours. "I've never seen her weep that hard," my aunt Celeste told me two decades later. "She just *wept*."

For many years, I wondered if my grandmother's sorrow stemmed from her first-born daughter leaving the nest, not from my mother's choices. Mommy always insisted it was the latter. "Milla, she was disappointed in me."

The discontentment and shame associated with my birth was difficult for me to accept in my early adult years. But I now understand that my grandma's feelings had less to do with my existence. It was about fear, honour, status, and respect, as is often the way in African families.

My grandmother had gotten married and had children at a young age. She wanted her eldest daughter to experience something different: to enjoy her twenties "with as much" freedom and independence as possible and set an example for her siblings by doing so. Now, my grandma wouldn't be able to live out her lifelong dream through her daughter and take pride in it. That's what crushed her.

In life, this type of projection can be damaging. It's something parents, even my own mother, are guilty of doing, as will I in time. It's about care and protection, which oftentimes can lead to control. And distrusting that children have been given the necessary tools to prosper in life, even when we stumble. As much as this behaviour can be in children's best interests, it isn't always about what we want and need to progress in our individual journeys. Sometimes, it's about what our parents want.

The thing about protection and control is that we, as human beings, only have access to so much of it. The parental need for control over children's pathways is what stifles them and parents, too. It forces kids to live up to their parents' standards, some of which are, at times, unrealistic and don't allow space or room for grace when we make mistakes. And it makes parents feel like failures when things don't pan out the way they envisioned. That's why releasing ourselves from parental expectations, regardless of how hard it is, is necessary. It will free us, along with our parents.

My mom indeed chose a different path from what my grandmother had wanted. That wasn't part of Grandma's plan, but it was part of the Creator's. You see, our life stories had already been written together. Nothing my grandma could say or do was going to alter that. I was always meant to come through this beautiful Black African woman—my mother's sacred womb.

Nineteen

CONNECTING THE DOTS

All of us are products of our childhood.

— Michael Jackson

"Get away from me!" Mom screamed.

"Stop it! PJ yanked my dad's shoulders.

"Did Marcus really put his hands on me?" Mommy asked herself.

It had started off as a relaxed, mellow evening. Dad was watching a football game, and Mom joined him on the black leather couch after laying me down to sleep. She made a comment about something small. To this day, she can't remember what it was. And my father got into a fit of rage.

"You're nothing! No man will ever want you because you have a baby. Your own family didn't want you."

Mom withdrew to the far side of the living room. Dad, then, jumped up and shoved her into the corner, his clenched fist in her face. "I'll harm you and take the baby if you leave me!"

It was only a couple months after I was born that my parents' relationship turned violent. They'd agreed that my mom should stay home and take care of me, but the strain of being the sole provider was getting to my father. And he became short-tempered for another reason: my mom's constant probing about a particular female friend.

"Who's that?" Mom would ask when he got off the phone.

"No one," he'd reply.

My mom never totally believed him. Her woman's intuition kept nagging at her. *He's lying*, she thought. *There's someone else.*

To make matters worse, my father was addicted to cannabis. When he came in after work, red-eyed, the stench of weed seeped from his clothes. Mom kept her distance. She couldn't stand the pungent, skunk-like odor.

At times, Dad would spend money on weed instead of paying rent. His financially irresponsible ways created problems not only with my mom but also with his own mother. She expected him to send money to her home country, Sierra Leone, the over-exploited mineral-wealthy country where my father was born and grew up until he moved to England at the age of twenty-four (eleven years before he would meet my mother) by himself. When she stopped receiving it, she blamed the new woman in her son's life. "She's keeping all the money for herself," my paternal grandmother told my dad. Even though her suspicions were the furthest thing from the truth, she grew to dislike my mother.

Roughly two years passed by, and the relationship between my mom and paternal grandmother was non-existent. So was ours. I've never met Grandma Asha, the lady from whom I inherited my Lebanese ancestry.

* * *

As time went on, things got worse between my parents. Often, they couldn't afford the rent, and so we moved around a lot. The three of us drove to Westminster in a dark green pearl metallic Nissan Altima and stayed there for a few weeks. We met some of my dad's relatives, and then visited my mom's father.

Papa greeted us warmly. "Bonjour, tout le monde!"

While my parents made small talk with my grandpa, he gleefully held me in his long, sturdy arms. "Now that you've made a family with my daughter, I want you to host a traditional gathering to celebrate this union and provide me with a $500 dowry."

"Okay," my father answered.

Thereafter we travelled to Southwark. We stayed at a place that my dad's friend owned. But that was short-lived, too.

Dad thought the next best solution for us was to stay with his sister, Ursula. She had a two-bedroom apartment in Bexley, and she also happened to be the only relative of my father's that my mom had formed a cordial relationship with. So, when Ursula agreed to let us room with her, we made our way southeast.

Throughout the first weeks, everything was fine. Ursula gave us a bedroom and made us feel welcomed. Mom would wake up early to start her shift as an assistant at a salon, while my dad, who disliked seeing me cry every time he would try taking me to a babysitter, kept an eye on me. He and I would stop by McDonald's to get chicken nuggets and fries sometimes, and tease and play with each other throughout the day.

But my mom soon found herself in the thick of sibling conflict. One afternoon, Dad and I picked Mom up from work, and a heated argument about money for a broken microwave erupted when we walked through the door. "You have to pay for a new one!" Ursula shouted.

"Okay, I'll replace it next week," Dad said.

"No, buy a new one now!"

Mom waited for the argument to fizzle out. A microwave was such a silly thing to fight over. But when Ursula grabbed a knife and pointed it towards her brother, my mom had to intervene.

"Stop!" she yelled.

"You're a whore!" Ursula responded.

"Don't speak to her like that," Dad shouted.

That, right there, was the ultimate betrayal in Ursula's eyes. Her own brother had sided with a "stranger" instead of standing by her side.

That night, my mom called her sister Celeste. My mom wanted me to stay at a well-balanced home until she and my father sorted themselves out. "Bring her over," Aunt Celeste agreed.

For the next five days, Auntie Celeste, who was living at her friend Keke's house, watched over me. She noticed that the sound of clinking pots and pans unnerved me. I'd curl up into a foetal position while lying in her lap. My aunt was shocked.

When things were calmer, Mom and Dad picked me up at Keke's house. I clung onto Mommy, not wanting to let her go when we reunited. We said our farewells to Auntie Celeste and Keke, and drove over to an apartment owned by my dad's cousin's girlfriend, Beatrice.

"You all can stay in the second room," she said.

My mom felt like we were in good hands. Living with Beatrice made us feel like a complete family again. Things were going noticeably well, too. Mom and Dad were getting along. Until they weren't.

One morning, everyone gathered at Beatrice's apartment for brunch. Andrew, dad's cousin who was going out with Beatrice, greeted us at the door. He was elated to see us.

While the adults chatted, Mommy held me in her arms, a comforting place for me. Dad caught up with his cousin, while Beatrice sat on the couch and Mom amused me.

"Come here! Come here!" Dad knelt and ushered me towards him.

I buried my head in Mom's shoulder. It was obvious to everyone that I didn't want to play with my father.

Dad glared at my mother. "She's been like this for a month! What have you been telling her?"

Everyone stood with their mouths wide open.

"You're telling her things about me! You're poisoning her! You're speaking French and you know I don't know it well!"

Dad lunged at my mother. "Stop!" Andrew and Beatrice shouted. They tried to pull my father away, but he wouldn't stop shoving her.

Kapow. For the first time in their relationship, my mom stood up for herself. She had enough of my father intimidating and threatening her. The force of my mom's punch was so hard that she gave my dad a black eye.

"Look what you did to me," he screamed.

"You guys stop!" Andrew and Beatrice pleaded.

My parents cooled down. But my dad's ego had been bruised as badly as his eye.

* * *

Two afternoons later, I jumped up and down on our bed as my mom folded laundry. "Weee!" Mommy and I were having a blast playing and laughing together.

Dad stormed into our bedroom, pinned Mom on the mattress, and wrapped his hands around her neck.

"Mommy! Mommy! Mommy!" I hollered. Her legs flailed in the air.

Beatrice rushed in, yelling. *"Stop it!"*

Mom got up, gasping for air. Then she grabbed me in her arms and huddled near Beatrice in the living room while my dad cut up every item he'd ever bought my mother.

"I can't do this anymore," my mom whispered.

We stayed close to Beatrice until nightfall, when both

she and my father left for work. Mom hastily packed up a small bag for the two of us. Then she called Keke.

"Can we stay with you?" Mom asked.

"Of course," Keke replied.

We left Beatrice's apartment that night and never returned. That was the last time my father laid a finger on my mother. And that was the last time father and daughter saw each other.

* * *

Being told *the story*, as the maternal side of my family saw it then, while I've matured has made me aware of where my first trauma and triggers were created. Right here—infancy. Witnessing abuse as a child has greatly affected me, consciously and subconsciously.

In my teenage years, I struggled to comprehend why my sympathetic nervous system, which is involved in the fight-or-flight response, would initiate when I heard loud noises or confrontations between people, or even myself and my brother. I'd have bubbling sensations in my stomach, a nauseating feeling, my shoulders would jump, or I'd experience intense emotions that made me want to run or sob.

Without a doubt, it was clear that the abusive environment I lived in impacted me when, twenty years later, Aunt Celeste revealed the defence mechanism I had formed. Hearing that I'd curl up in a ball when I was afraid not only shocked me, it also gave me a better understanding of myself. It was one of those "Ah-ha" moments for me. I learned that this early life experience contributed to the formation of a big part of my identity and personality.

I ascertained that I became so conditioned to loud noises that my mind and body couldn't differentiate between seeing and hearing an actual threat—abuse—and an ordinary noise. It is an important correlation between baby me and grown up me. One that breaks my heart.

Equally, it hurts me to know that my father accused my mother of telling me, a fourteen-month-old, unfavourable things about him. In my dad's mind, the only reason why I stopped wanting to be in his presence was because of my mom. But, when Mommy told me this information, I intuited that the root cause of my sudden change in behaviour towards my dad was much deeper than that.

Innately, infants gravitate towards their mothers. They carry us in their wombs, and thereafter, babies rely on them for nourishment, so their attachment remains strong. That's also why I didn't like being away from my mom during those five days she had left me with Aunt Celeste. I don't fault her for making that decision. It was wise, considering the chaos in Ursula's house. But going from seeing my mom every day to not seeing her at all made me feel disconnected from her and abandoned.

On top of that, children are always protective of their mothers, especially Black mothers. That need to protect my mama is something I would only identify later on in my life with the help of my therapist. Seeing my mom physically hurt and crying at such a young age has left a lasting imprint on me. I instantly go into protective mode if I feel she's being mistreated. In my eyes, I am more than her daughter. I am her protector. I am her keeper. She is my *everything*.

All of this is why, over time, I preferred not to be around my father dispite our closeness. I no longer felt a sense of safety or protection around him, the first man who loved me. It didn't matter if his intentions towards me were in the right place. "He loved playing with you," Mom says. "You were wanted by him. You were his princess. He loved you. He doted on you."

In those last days we shared together during my infancy as a family, the hard truth is, both of my parents failed me.

* * *

During the following weeks, my mom asked mutual friends of hers and my dad not to divulge details about our whereabouts to maintain peace and sanity. But, after a short period of time, my dad's friend Perry reached out to her. My mom was surprised to hear from him.

"Marcus regrets losing you," he told her. "He's sorry about what happened."

Mom was unmoved. "Did he tell you what really happened?"

Perry had no idea.

"It's time for me to change the direction of my life," Mommy said.

"I totally understand," Perry replied. He never contacted her again.

Even though my mom declined to reconcile with my dad, there were rumours of him being seen around the complex we were living in, asking for us. Keke's older sister told Mom two things: "He doesn't look well," and "Keep going forward." That's what we did.

While all of this took place, my maternal grandma, Aunt Felicia, and uncles Luke and Rick immigrated to Canada. Canadian immigration was more sympathetic towards my family being refugees. When my grandma and Felicia found out about what had occurred between my mom and dad, they encouraged my mom to come to Canada too.

Mom agreed. Uprooting to Canada seemed like a good opportunity for us to have a second chance at building a promising life. So, she was eager to move quickly.

With assistance from my aunt Celeste and my grandma, we, including Auntie Celeste, made it to Canada, where we met up with the rest of our family. I don't know where Mommy and I would have found ourselves if not for them. We were blessed to have had their help. That's what family is for, right?

The agonizing part about all of this is that my grandfather, who I've dedicated my book to, died due to complications with diabetes on his way to Canada. Papa made it as far as New York City. At the time, no one was aware of just how sick he was. I gather he didn't want anyone to know the truth about his condition. Old school African men loved to hold onto their pride for as long as they could.

Out of all the Kabongo grandchildren that now exist, I was the only one he ever met. I don't recollect meeting him with my mother and father during our trip to Westminster. I was far too young. But one thing I know for certain is that we adored each other.

"Papa! Papa!" I'd say, giggling over the phone with him before he entered Heaven's gates. Hearing that story from Auntie Celeste never fails to bring a smile to my face. It's a sweet reminder of the love we once physically shared.

* * *

Mommy and I arrived in Aurora in July 1999 and moved into my grandma's new place on Bellarosa Lane. A few days later, she and my mom sat on white lawn chairs in the front yard and talked. "You look like you're pregnant," Grandma said with a gaze as intense as that hot summer day.

"No ... it's not possible," Mom explained. "I'm on birth control."

"You can still get pregnant with those things," my grandmother replied.

Grandma bought my mom a pregnancy test at the local drugstore. "Well, what does it say?" she asked.

My mom glanced at the test. Her mother, the ever-observant nurse, was correct. She was pregnant again.

The news came as a big surprise to Mommy. She thought that she just had some random weight gain. But the OBG-YN informed her that she was five months pregnant.

In a matter of months, I not only lost the first man who had loved me, I'd also gained a brother who would come to love me. My life underwent a turbulent transformation as the family of two expanded to a family of three again. While the opposite occurred for my father, a man who I can now see tried his best despite all the betrayal, pressure, and rejection he had faced from both his own family and my maternal family, but who also let his inner turmoil consume him, leading to severe mistakes that altered his relationships with my mom, me, and a baby boy who came to be. To this day, my father has no clue that he shares a son with my mother too.

Twenty

A LETTER TO MY FATHER

Nearly half of all Black children live in single-parent households.

— U.S. Department of Justice
Statistic 2023

One December morning, I woke up to the sound of sniffling. I walked to the dining room and saw Mom sitting at the table. She had a tissue in her hand. "Were you crying?"

"Oh, I'm fine," she said. When Mom had wept, that was her usual response, an unbelievable one.

"No, you aren't. I can tell you were crying."

Mom exhaled deeply. "I was thinking about your father."

That wasn't surprising. Dad seemed to appear in my mother's thoughts many times throughout the years. She must've been ruminating about my dad when she asked Jonathan and me how we felt about him shortly before my sixteenth birthday. I didn't know what to think until she gave me some of the missing puzzle pieces.

On the day of my high school graduation, Mom brought up Dad's name, too. "Your dad was on my mind." She paused. "He's missed a lot."

Mom was right—my dad had missed a lot. It would have been nice to have him at my graduation ceremony, such an important milestone in my life. But I brushed off my mother's comments without a second thought. Talking about my father was the last thing I wanted to do.

"Mom, it's okay," I said, rubbing her back. "Don't worry about it."

But for whatever reason, during the past few years, the month of December seemed to make my mom dewy-eyed about my dad. Perhaps it was because December was the final month of the year and symbolized endings and beginnings, making people reflect. Or it was because families typically gathered together.

Mom would bring Dad up, and instantly, I'd find myself in an uneasy space. My dad had been the villain in my mom's story, but in mine, he wasn't. As much as he had scarred both my mother and me, he had never harmed me, physically.

Feeling the heaviness of my mom's emotional state would leave me asking these questions: *How do I discuss and respond to how I feel about my father? How do I express my pain to my mother? How do I help console my only parent, who hates the other?*

Children who grow up in households with domestic violence feel as if we have to choose a side. Often, we feel a duty to protect the abused parent. I feared saying something triggering or "wrong" to my mom. I didn't even know what to say to her at times. All I knew was that when I heard my mother's aching heart, it became harder for me to give a voice to mine.

The way I saw it, Mommy bringing up my father was necessary. I would be given the opportunity to discuss how his absence in my life has affected me. But it was unhelpful because I had to set my feelings aside and comfort her.

Mom would shake her head. "Out of all the suitors I had, I chose him. I heard it a thousand times … I fucked up in my choice of mates!" No one had ever told her directly that she had messed up. But in all the venom-filled words from her relatives throughout the years, that message could be heard.

Hearing my mom's words would make the thick walls that surrounded my daddy wound close. I could sense the deep guilt within my mother, especially as she scoured the web to find my father so that I could reconnect with him and Jonathan could finally meet him. I felt awful knowing that she kept reaching an impasse and that there was nothing I could do to help her, to help me find the most painful missing piece in my story.

However, contrary to what my mom thought, I didn't think it was necessary for her to beat herself up about not being able to find our dad or having chosen him. I do believe that we, as women, have to make better decisions about the men we choose to bear children for. As my brother often says, "A child is the *highest* honour a woman can give a man." So it's up to us to use discernment while vetting men before we create life with them. We choose our mates.

It is also up to us to be mindful of how our decisions as women can affect our children. I, in no way, believe that my parents should have remained together. Their relationship was too volatile. But, as women, we too often allow our emotions to take precedence over our decision-making. As my father figure Tony has told me, "Every child has a right to know their parents." And despite everything that occurred between my parents, I now know that I deserved the right to be in communication with my father too.

Despite all of this, I just felt the situation was unfortunate. Mommy was young when she had crossed paths with my father, who was slightly over a decade older than her. At nineteen, how many of us make great choices in our love lives?

There was no need for Mom to have a negative viewpoint, because as far as I was concerned, if my father was a mistake, then so was I. And I knew that my mom thought of her children as a blessing. To me, it was simple: this was how her story was meant to be. Sandra and Marcus were destined to meet. And this was how *my* story was meant to be, too.

On that December day, I told Mommy that she needed to forgive herself and him. Holding onto regret was keeping her trapped. I wanted my mom to free herself from that.

It's taken my mom time, but with help from therapy, she's learning to forgive Marcus for the past and prays for him now. Wherever my father is, my mother truly wishes him well.

* * *

The year before I moved to 111 Transition Road was the last time I dreamt about my dad. We were sitting around a table at a restaurant, talking. Both of us were calm and relaxed. That's all I can remember.

That spring day, I awoke to chirping birds and teary eyes. As I wiped away each falling tear, I told myself, *It's time to heal from Dad.*

All my life it has been easy to pretend I am fine without my father, but the truth is that my heart hurts because I don't have him. These dreams occurred throughout the years to remind me of that. I could pretend that my father's absence didn't affect me during each passing day, but my subconscious brought the truth to the forefront of my mind. So, that day, I promised myself that I'd begin to heal from my daddy wound when I found stillness in my life and mind.

Now, here I am, in a place where I have immense peace, and have garnered enough strength to talk about the forbidden topic—my father. This time, I choose to heal by looking *within*, instead of searching for answers about him like I had been doing since I was six years old.

The Letter

Dear Dad,

Or should I say Marcus? To tell you the truth, for the longest time, I've had difficulty referring to you as Dad. I felt that you hadn't earned that title in my life, so I didn't know what to call you. Dad? Daddy? Father? Marcus?

Dad … I've struggled with your absence in my life for a very long time. I've wondered who you are, what you are, and where you are. I've constantly been in search of details about the man who helped create me. The man who, for so long, I was told that I looked like. But as I get older, I realize how much searching for you has hurt me.

You are my deepest wound. Not having you in my life has meant that I didn't feel unconditionally loved, protected, worthy, cared for, and wanted by you. Most of all, not having you in my life has made me feel abandoned.

At times, I've wondered if you looked hard enough to find me. And if you didn't, why not? I've wondered if you'd accept me. I've wondered … And still through all that wondering I'm left with nothing. Nothing but broken pieces.

I want you to know that I forgive you for giving me those broken pieces that I've now pieced together to make me whole again. I forgive you for falling short. For missing so many important moments in my life: parent-teacher nights, basketball games, my sweet sixteen, my high school and university graduations, and my biggest accomplishments yet to come …

I want you to know that I understand you did the best that you could at that time in your life. I want you to know that, although I wish you had done better by me and my mother during those last weeks/days when I was little, I'm releasing myself from that pain and accepting that we might never get an apology for your detrimental actions on the last day we saw each other. And I want you to know that despite everything, Mom, Jonathan (who you've never met), and I have made it! The little girl you were so adamant to name, Jamilla, turned into a warrior!

I want you to know that a part of me will always love you, and a part of me will always be open to reconciliation. But only if that's part of God's plan. I've surrendered that to the Most High now. And if it is not, I thank you for helping me become the woman I am today. I have a feeling you'd be proud!

I wish you nothing but the best wherever you are. I love you.

Your daughter,
Jamilla

Twenty-One

A LOVE MESSAGE TO MYSELF

Wanna fly, you got to give up the shit that weighs you down.

— Toni Morrison

*T*his three-year writing journey would reveal to me, yet again, that I had been looking back on my life through a surface-level lens. I had believed that my childhood trauma was created in Caledon, the city where my world had been upturned. I wanted to write a story about healing from those wounds, but instead ended up with a story about my father.

Now I understand that the first twenty-six years of my life have revolved around him. The other half of me—my dad—has been and will always be a part of the story, but he's no longer a secret. I've freed him and me.

The one thing that hasn't changed is my purpose in writing this memoir. As I see it, healing is the process of becoming less emotionally attached to an experience. It doesn't mean your heart won't ache, or you won't feel negative emotions when you think of a memory. There are times when you will. The emotions will simply appear less intensely with time.

When they don't, find your healthy outlet. I'd lay out my yoga mat and write letters to people: my father, mother, grandmother, and relatives after completing a chapter that angered me. Or I'd bend down on my knees and ask the Universal Creator to help me let go of my emotional attachment to an experience or individual.

Learning to accept, learn, heal, and move forward isn't meant to happen overnight. For some, it's a process that can take a lifetime.

I'll admit that I don't have everything figured out. That would make life boring, and who wants that?

What I do know is that faith and spirituality have guided me throughout my healing journey. As a child, I didn't fully comprehend my mother's affinity towards gospel music. Mommy would turn on the television in the living room every Sunday morning and call us over. "You guys, we're going to watch Bobby Jones Gospel on the BET channel." Then I'd see Shirley Caesar, The Clark Sisters, or Kirk Franklin hop on stage with their choirs and sing.

Mom clapped and rejoiced in front of the TV while I wondered, *Why is she making me watch this?* I sensed that listening to gospel music was an integral part of my mom's being. It had gotten her, and later the three of us, through the most trying times in our lives. She wanted gospel music, and more importantly, the Creator, to be a part of my being too.

Thankfully, they both are now, just in a different way. I've found healing and connection to the Most High through meditation.

* * *

Undeniably, with each passing day, I hope to continue growing and learning how to heal from my wounds: the daddy, mama, grandma, and the list goes on. But I don't want my father's absence in my life or my past to define me. So, I've written a love message to myself and ... *you.*

Intuition. What a powerful tool we have from the Divine. Following it is what has led me to the place where I am today. Living in purpose and peace.

Blessed? That's not even a question at this point. Gratitude for everything that has been given to me for allowing myself to be divinely guided.

Healing. That's what has brought me to this place of lightness. It's all thanks to the Creator and every single person (you know who you are) who has helped me along the way.

How did I get here? I ask. The answer is simple but oftentimes hard in life: unconditional love. To exert the truest form of love, I had to find something key within myself first: self-love.

Accepting that I am a fallible human being, that I've made and will make mistakes to teach me what not to do, and that the flaws I have exist so that I can evolve has helped me understand the concept of forgiveness. Because I've done wrong and needed to not only give myself grace but ask for grace during moments of my life, I've learned to extend it to others. So past offenses no longer hold me hostage. They don't belong to me.

I have set myself free.

I am now at peace with the past life experiences that the Creator wanted me to go through to obtain lessons.

And I am proud of myself for having the courage to heal from the events that have molded me. The experiences that have sculpted me. The times that both tested and facilitated the evolution of my beauty, resiliency, and strength. The moments that seemed so unbearable but proved to be a prerequisite for my ascension. These chapters of my life are what I am now grateful for.

Now, when I look into the rear-view mirror, I don't see a lost, fatherless daughter navigating life while forgetting to water the most important seed: herself.

I see a confident Queen with infinite strength and steadfast belief in the power of her light, which she is using to inspire generations through her work. Work that she hopes will encourage people to heal from their childhood wounds, connect with their inner beings, and remind them to do the things they've always loved. Like taking long walks on the beach, riding their favourite bike, breathing in the smell of fresh air, soaking in the blazing sun, watching white butterflies fly, or looking at the blossoming leaves.

And my hope for myself is to not fear, to continue to flow with the water, release control, and surrender my life to the Most High.

Detach from experiences and people who no longer serve me. For now that I am walking in line with my purpose, I no longer need them to teach me things. But I thank each person endlessly.

Believe who is meant for me will be for me.

Trust that everything always works out in the end.

Continue to still my mind through meditation.

Paint anything my soul desires: the skyline from my condo, a heart, or a Fulani (the beautiful tribe of my paternal grandfather) print.

Positively affirm myself.

Vent to my loved ones and therapist.

Allow myself to cry.

Be present. Be open.

Worry less.

And listen to my intuition. That's where my Divine guidance lies.

In all, I accept that I cannot change my childhood, nor can you, but what we can do is change the way we cope with our traumas. I, along with you, can either choose to project onto people, and damage them and myself. Or we can all continue to look internally so that we don't let our triggers determine what our futures will look and feel like.

I promise to not let my past define me.

I choose to heal, even when I'm old and grey.
I choose light and love.

I choose to put my spiritual, emotional, mental, and physical well-being first.

And I vow to create balance, harmony, and positivity in my life. For as long as the Universal Light Creator wants me on this Earth, that's what it will want me to do.

My journey here and beyond will forever remain to be continued ...

Mommy, Jonathan, and I in the present day.

*In a world filled with hate, we must still dare to hope.
In a world filled with anger, we must still dare to comfort. In a world filled with despair, we must still dare to
dream. And in a world filled with distrust, we must still
dare to believe.*

— Michael Jackson

Less than one year after the release of my memoir, my beloved
father and I reunited. ♥

ACKNOWLEDGEMENTS

First and foremost, I'd like to thank the Creator for not only bestowing me with such a huge task, one that has taken me on a beautiful journey that I continue to be amazed by, but for also providing me with the strength to see it through. I hope that I've made you proud.

Mama, my queen, without you there would be no me. I'm so thankful for your words of wisdom throughout my life and for supporting me every step of the way during the making of *The Glow Up*. Thank you for being brave enough to tell me your story and for having faith in me to convey our life journey together with Jonathan to the world. Je t'aime beaucoup!

My big little brother, Jonathan, I thank you for your words of wisdom and support during this process. It truly means the world to me. I hope you are proud of this book. I love you!

My beloved daddy, thank you for not giving up on finding Jonathan and me, for loving me unconditionally, and for always keeping me in your heart and in your prayers. Thank you for supporting me. I love you!!!

My day ones, Mrs. B, therapist, and Apple family, thank you all for your continuous support, love & care.

To the people who've allowed me to use their quotes, thank you for your generosity.

Ian Keteku, thank you for being my first editor, for recognizing the power of my story that I had not fully grasped, and for helping me with the Canada Council for the Arts grant.

Ellie Barton, my line editor, words cannot express the gratitude I have for you! You mentored me, taught me the craft of writing, devoted ample time to my book, and helped me bring my story to life in a way that I could never have imagined. You are an editing queen!

Canada Council for the Arts, thank you for supporting me with a grant that helped me research the effects of generational trauma on Black/first generation youth in North America.

BIBLIOGRAPHY

Angelou, Maya. Rainbow in the Cloud: The Wisdom and Spirit of Maya Angelou. New York: Random House, 2014.

Austin, Daryl. "6 Reasons Why Yelling at Kids Doesn't Actually Work." Parents. parents.com/health/ healthy-happy-kids/a-parental-wake-up-call-yelling-doesnt-help/.

Bruce, Debra Fulghum. "Exercise and Depression: Endorphins, Reducing Stress, and More." WebMD. www.webmd.com/depression/guide/ exercise-depression.

Confucius. The Analects of Confucius: a Philosophical Translation. New York: Ballantine Books, 1999.

Divorce Court. "Full Episode- Bolton vs. Mitchell: #ChildsPlay." YouTube. www.youtube.com/ watch?v=VNdc4AB7Kbs.

Doig, Ivan. Excerpt from The Whistling Season.
    Orlando: Harcourt, 2006.

Fraga, Juli. "Being 'Highly Sensitive' Is a Real Trait.
    Here's What It Feels Li." Healthline. www.
    healthline.com/health/mental-health/what-its-
    like-highly-sensitive-person-hsp.

Gross, Terry. "How 'modern-Day Slavery' in the Congo
    Powers the Rechargeable Battery Economy."
    NPR. www.npr.org/sections/
    goatsandsoda/2023/02/01/1152893248/red-
    cobalt-congo-drc-mining-siddharth-kara.

Higuera, Valencia. "Brain Fog: 6 Potential Causes."
    Healthline. www.healthline.com/health/brain-
    fog.

Horne, Lena. Press release. www.halifaxcc.edu/
    halifacts/PressRel/2018/02082018a.htm.

Justice, National Center for Juvenile. "Living
    Arrangements of Children by Race/Ethnicity."
    Living arrangements of children by Race/
    ethnicity, 1970-2023. www.ojjdp.gov/ojstatbb//
    population/qa01202.asp?qaDate=2023.

Kara, Siddharth. Cobalt red how the blood of the Congo
    Powers Our Lives. New York, N.Y: St. Martin's
    Press, 2023.

Key, Ellen. "Child Labour and Child Crimes ." Essay.
    In The Century of the Child, 327–327, 1909.

Koyenikan, Idowu. Wealth for all: Living a life of success at the edge of your ability. Fuquay-Varina, NC: Grandeur Touch, LLC, 2016.

"Lauren London on: Trauma, Spirituality & How to Recover from Loss." YouTube. www.youtube.com/watch?v=Fbv8jJ_ccNI.

Mbeko, Patrick, and N'Gbanda Honoré Nzambo-ko-Atumba. Stratégie du Chaos et du Mensonge: Poker menteur en afrique des grands lacs. Québec, Canada: Éditions de l'Erablière, 2014.

Mbeko, Patrick. Guerre secrète en Afrique Centrale: Comment les états-unis et la France se sont affrontés dans la région des grands lacs. Saint-Denis: Kontre kulture, 2015.

Mbeko, Patrick. Le Canada dans les guerres en Afrique centrale: Génocides et Pillages des ressources minières du Congo par le Rwanda Interposé. Montréal: Le Nègre éditeur, 2012.

"Memory Development." Tākai. www.takai.nz/find-resources/articles/memory-development/#:~:text=Explicit%20.

"Michael Jackson - Oxford Union Speech (March 6th, 2001)." YouTube. www.youtube.com/watch?v=PkElyPTY1u8.

Michel, Thierry. Mobutu, King of Zaire: An African Tragedy. The Quest for Power. Brooklyn, NY: Icarus Films, 2000. http://docuseek2.com/if-mob1.

Micu, Alexandru. "Your First Memory Is Probably
        Older than You Think." ZME Science. www.
        zmescience.com/science/first-memories-earlier-
        than-believed-9426363/.

Morrison, Toni. "Chapter 8." Essay. In Song of
        Solomon, 179. New York: Vintage International.
        Vintage Books, a division of Penguin Random
        House LLC, 2019.

Onana, Charles. Holocauste au Congo: L'omerta de la
        communauté internationale. Paris: L'Artilleur,
        2023.

Péan, Pierre. Noires fureurs, Blancs Menteurs: Rwanda
        1990-1994. Paris: Fayard, 2014.

Pichardo. "Stress, Anxiety, and IBS: Stress Relief,
        Anxiety Treatment, and More." WebMD. www.
        webmd.com/ibs/stress-anxiety-ibs.

"Pruning in Three Steps." Pruning in Three Steps, a
        Pictorial - Gardening Solutions - University of
        Florida, Institute of Food and Agricultural
        Sciences. www.gardeningsolutions.ifas.ufl.edu/
        care/pruning/pruning-three-steps.html.

Rever, Judi. In Praise of Blood: The Crimes of the
        Rwandan Patriotic Front. Random House
        Canada, 2018.

"Sarah Baartman - a Freak Show Attraction, Timeline, Personal Life - Sarah Baartman Biography." Famousbio. famousbio.net/sarah-baartman-3805.html#carousel-slide0.

"Selah Marley Calls out Lauryn Hill and Rohan Marley for Having a Challenging Upbringing." YouTube. www.youtube.com/watch?v=1_Cxbr1ztUQ.

"Sometimes 'Glowing up' Is Ugly 😫 | Health, Wealth & Boundaries; the Truth about 'Levelling Up.'" YouTube. www.youtube.com/watch?v=shce6YfBGI4.

Stillman, Jessica. "The Science of Lying: The More You Do It, the Easier It Gets - Inc.Com." Inc. www.inc.com/jessica-stillman/the-science-of-lying-more-you-do-it-easier-it-gets.html.

WebMD Editorial Contributors. "The Connection between IBS & Depression." WebMD. www.webmd.com/ibs/irritable-bowel-syndrome-ibs-depression.